THE LONG RUN

THE LONG RUN

Eric Mackenzie Robertson from the Battle of the Somme to the Olympics

JOAN SULLIVAN

P.O. Box 2188, St. John's, NL, Canada, A1C 6E6
WWW.BREAKWATERBOOKS.COM

LIBRARY AND ARCHIVES CANADA CATALOGUING IN PUBLICATION
Sullivan, Joan, 1963-
The long run / Joan Sullivan.
Includes bibliographical references.
ISBN 978-1-55081-610-5 (paperback)

1. Robertson, Eric Mackenzie, 1892-1975. 2. Great Britain. Army. Royal Newfoundland Regiment--Biography. 3. World War, 1914-1918--Canada--Biography. 4. Olympic athletes--Newfoundland and Labrador--Biography. 5. Long-distance runners--Newfoundland and Labrador--Biography. 6. Newfoundland and Labrador--Biography.
I. Title.
FC2173.1.R63S85 2015 971.8 C2015-904891-5

Breakwater Books acknowledges the support of the Canada Council for the Arts, which last year invested $153 million to bring the arts to Canadians throughout the country. We acknowledge the financial support of the Government of Canada and the Government of Newfoundland and Labrador through the Department of Tourism,Culture and Recreation for our publishing activities.

PRINTED AND BOUND IN CANADA.

Canada Council for the Arts | Conseil des Arts du Canada
Canada
Newfoundland Labrador

DEDICATION

Timothy Patrick Sullivan
February 3, 1968-September 3, 1972

&

Christopher Michael Sullivan
December 3, 1964-March 10, 2003

We remember.

The Army and Navy Club,
Pall Mall, London, S. W. 1.

Dear Robertson,

Thank you very much for your letter. I am always ready to take my hat off to a really good sportsman and you are certainly one of the best I have met. And not only in the running track have you proved yourself a good sportsman, but also on the battlefield, where you were wounded whilst "playing the greatest game of all" \viz. fighting for your team. I hope we shall meet again. If not, the best of luck to you wherever you may be.

Yours sincerely,
R. J. Kentish

CONTENTS

CHAPTER ONE

The Greatest Game of All

THE 1916 OLYMPICS never took place. But they still exist.

Officially known as the Games of the VI Olympiad, they were scheduled to be held in Berlin, Germany, in the summer of 1916. Due to the outbreak of World War I, they were eventually cancelled.[1] But because the Olympic Games are numbered according to the Olympiad, a four-year period as certain as the march of time, the Olympiad still progresses even if the competitions themselves are not held.[2]

Berlin was selected as the host city during the 14th International Olympic Committee Session in Stockholm on July 4, 1912. The city defeated bids from Alexandria, Amsterdam, Brussels, Budapest, and Cleveland. French Baron Pierre de Coubertin, the IOC's second president, hoped that awarding the games to Berlin might staunch some of that country's growing militarism, and avert looming hostilities.[3]

Germany was not the only nation adhering to this increasingly martial state of mind. The idea that war was the answer

1 David Miller, *The Official History of the Olympic Games and the IOC* (Edinburgh: Mainstream Publishing, 2012), 28 & 71.

2 David E. Martin and Roger W.H. Gynn, *The Olympic Marathon* (Champaign, Ill: Human Kinetics, 2000), 96.

3 Miller, *The Official History*, 28 & 71.

to a lot of problems was gaining traction in several European governments, especially in the latter half of the 1900s.

Germany's provocative mentality actually aspired to ancient Olympic ideals: participation in the Olympics, just like participation in war, was a nation-definer, and Germany had just been unified in 1871. Its bid for the games had been pugnaciously impressive, with marching parades and the promise of a new stadium, over which would fly de Coubertin's new Olympic flag with its Delphic-inspired rings.

In Germany, military thought was infused throughout its political policy and stoked increased investment in armaments and mobilization. The German Army was called a "State within a State" and was absolutely complicit in the deteriorating international situation.

But many other nations were increasingly belligerent. Britain was rapidly weening its foreign policy off appeasement.[4] Austria-Hungary, Italy, Russia, France, and Britain all pumped up their military expenditures. The naval arms race between Germany and Britain had doubled the German battle fleet and produced the first British dreadnought (literally "fear nothing"), which was bigger, faster, and brandished with more firepower than anything else at sea. (Although it would be the weapons introduced and enhanced during the war—like gas, submarines, and tanks—combined with anachronistic or unproven battle strategies, that so massively extended the First World War's destructive power.)[5]

Still, Germany did not neglect preparations for the Olympics. Work on the Deutsches Stadion, "German Stadium," began in 1912 at what was the Grunewald Race Course. Its capacity was 18,000. On June 8, 1913, the stadium was dedicated with the release of 10,000 pigeons flying over the 60,000 in attendance.

4 Niall Ferguson, *The Pity of War* (New York: Basic Books, 1999), 55.

5 Dan Todman, *The Great War: Myth and Memory* (London: Hambledon and London, 2005), 3.

Program details were being finalized at the IOC Congress in Paris when word came that Austro-Hungarian Archduke Franz Ferdinand had been assassinated.[6]

Even this news, in itself, did not affect the planning process. No one foresaw catastrophe. Indeed, even after Austro-Hungary declared war against Serbia on July 28, causing Russia to mobilize in Serbia's defence, and Germany invaded Belgium and Luxembourg and set their sights on France, causing Britain to declare war on Germany on August 4,[7] organization for the 1916 Olympics carried on, as no one expected the hostilities would continue for many months, let alone several years. None of the Allied or Central Powers, with the exception of Austro-Hungary, had a direct stake in the Balkan unrest that led Yugoslav nationalist Gavrilo Princip to open fire on the archduke and his wife, Sophie, Duchess of Hohenberg.

The early twentieth century was studded with similar crises. The fortunes of small states were often dice cast by greater nations. Still the power-wielding nations had always managed to cope with and contain the entanglements (or at least postpone the consequences for another day).

But not this time. Negotiations buckled under the weight of Germany's bellicose, rigid demands and unchecked mobilization.[8] With the German invasions of late summer, an international conflict erupted. Still, all involved anticipated a short, decisive campaign.

During the first month and even into the second year of the war, the Germans, along with most everyone else, continued

6 Miller, *The Official History*, 72.

7 The Ottoman Empire joined the Central Powers in November 1914, and Bulgaria in 1915. Italy joined the Allies in 1915, Romania in 1916, and the United States in 1917.

8 Kaiser Wilhelm of Germany to Tsar Nicolas II of Russia, "The Willy-Nicky Telegrams," in *World War 1 Reader*, ed. Michael S. Neiberg, (New York: New York UP, 2007), 88.

to expect the fighting to conclude quickly. German athletes were keenly interested in American coaching and training techniques and kept up with their studies in preparation for competition. A four-man team had been dispatched to tour American university campuses and military schools.[9] The IOC carried on their own work as well, wrangling with the renewed commitment to amateurism (they had just demanded Jim Thorpe, the American sportsman considered one of the most versatile in the world, return his medals for playing two seasons of semi-professional baseball before competing in the pentathlon and decathlon). They were also considering a proposal (from Canada, among other countries) to establish a Winter Games.[10]

When it did become apparent that the war would in fact last much longer than most people anticipated, and certainly through 1916, six cities in the US—which was still isolated from the war—offered to host the Olympics: Chicago, Cleveland, Newark, New York, Philadelphia, and San Francisco. There was concern over interrupting the cycle; the modern games had only restarted in 1896, twenty years before. But the German Olympic Committee held firm to their city's nomination.[11] And de Coubertin, who, though he was fifty-one, had enlisted in the French army, supported them, writing,

> The IOC has not the right to withdraw the celebration of the Olympic Games from the country to which the celebration has been given without consulting that country. The VIth Olympic Games remain and will remain credited to Berlin but it is possible they will not be held. In olden times it happened that it was not

9 Miller, *The Official History*, 72.

10 Miller, *The Official History*, 72. Thorpe's medals were restored in 1983, thirty years after his death.

11 John R. Gold and Margaret M. Gold eds, *Olympic Cities: City Agendas, Planning and the World's Games, 1896–2012* (London: Routledge, 2007), 27.

> possible to celebrate the Games but they did not for this reason cease to exist.[12]

De Coubertin also refused to eject Germany from the IOC, resulting in the British representative's resignation, although he did move the IOC's offices to Lausanne, in neutral Switzerland.[13]

And the war continued.

The German Stadium stood empty, and the Games, if not the Olympiad, were cancelled.

In July 1916, young men from around the world were engaged on a different field.

12 Miller, *The Official History*, 73.

13 Ibid., 72.

CHAPTER TWO

A Good Sportsman

ERIC MACKENZIE ROBERTSON was born September 12, 1892, the year of The Great Fire, in St. Johns, Newfoundland. He was the only surviving son of Lucy M. and John R. Robertson; they also had four daughters: Ethel, Evelyn, Stella, and Lorna.

John Robertson owned a clothing store at 296-298 Water Street. He carried high-end men's wear and was the St. John's agent for several lines based in England, Scotland, and Ireland, such as Hollands Mill, Samuel Martin Co., and George Bubeck. This was the family business Eric would join after finishing school.

Robertson, though Protestant (the family was Presbyterian), enrolled at the Catholic school St. Bonaventure's when he was sixteen. Many non-Catholics attended St Bon's for the school's excellent scholastic reputation. As a student, Robertson ran in track and field and long distance with the Newfoundland Highlanders, a Presbyterian-sponsored boys' brigade. Such cadet teams raced each other in inter-brigade tournaments; this was the core of youth sports in the city at the time. At seventeen he placed fourth in a fifteen-mile race. Still, this activity was not primarily competitive for young Eric Robertson. He never considered himself a great athlete, and mostly ran for sheer enjoyment, but his athleticism would later serve his country well.

The Robertson's house was on Maxse Street, a short, pretty street running east-west in the Georgetown neighborhood of downtown St. John's. The street is named for former Newfoundland governor Sir Henry Fitzhardinge Maxse, who "did the residence [Government House] an honour by being the only governor to expire within its walls, and was the first to die in office since Pickmore."[14]

It was, and is, a good street, a desirable address. The 1921 census displays the family names Devine, Jardine, Collins, Dooley, Brocklehurst, Kearney, Rose, Stevens, Peet, Murphy, Green, Taylor, Oldfield, Carter, Oliphant (as well as the given names of various servants: Annas and Ariannas, Charlottes and Brides, Bridgets and Mays).[15]

The census also shows that many of the children listed, in 1921, are daughters, hinting at the attrition of WWI. The sons had enlisted in the Regiment, and the war enveloped them.

All the neighbourhoods of St. John's offered up their young men to the war effort, but Maxse Street would prove particularly bereaved. The three Taylor brothers of number 5 Maxse were all lost within a single year, and their bodies never found. Their headstone in the General Protestant Cemetery, between Old Topsail and Waterford Bridge Road, paraphrases a line of poetry by Rupert Brooke and reads, "There is one spot of France that is forever Britain." Of the six young men who enlisted from Maxse Street, only two returned.[16]

[14] Paul O'Neill, *The Oldest City* (St. John's: Boulder Publications, 2003), 108.

[15] Kevin Major, personal interview, 26 June 2014.

[16] Major, personal interview.

Eric Robertson, of 3 Maxse Street, enlisted in the Newfoundland Regiment on September 7, 1914—five days before he turned twenty-two—at the CLB Armoury on Harvey Road. His occupation was listed as clerk, his annual salary $600. The Terms of Service were "Duration of war." His Regimental number was #497. This made him one of the First Five Hundred (the number was actually 537), one of the celebrated "Blue Puttees."

All told, 1460 men from the city of St. John's would enlist, 365 of them would be killed, and 352 discharged for injury.

CHAPTER THREE

You Must Be Ready For This

ON THE EVENING of August 4, 1914, the Governor of Newfoundland, Walter Davidson, received a cable informing him that Britain was at war with Germany. The relay of information was thus: HMS *Calypso* Lt.-Commander A. MacDermott brought to Davidson, at Government House, a cable received at 6:30 pm which read, "The War telegram will be issued at midnight (London time) authorizing you to commence hostilities against Germany. But in view of terms of our ultimatum they may decide to open fire at any moment. You must be ready for this." Newfoundland, as a British colony, would officially be at war. A further message at 9:25 pm, from the British secretary of state for the colonies, Lewis Harcourt, simply confirmed, "War has broken out with Germany."[17]

The Legislature was not called together to pass its own resolution. Instead, politicians from all sides (Edward Patrick Morris's People's Party, Robert Bond's Liberals, and William Coaker's Fishermen's Protective Union) met in a special session of the Legislature to determine what going to war meant for Newfoundland. In short order, all hands were in

17 Barb Sweet, "Service Monday will remember the arrival of 1914 war telegram," *The Telegram* (August 2, 2014) A9.

the fold: "This is not a time when we should think of Party differences," said John Kent, "This is a time when our land calls for united action!"[18]

By August 8, Davidson wired London that Newfoundland would raise five hundred men for land service and one thousand for naval service. The Prime Minister, Morris, approved this decision, again without consulting the Legislature.

Four days later, on August 12, 1914, there was a public meeting of citizens in St. John's. They too approved the turn of events and passed a motion that led to the creation of what was soon named the Patriotic Association of Newfoundland. This committee would oversee the recruitment, training, and outfitting of the Newfoundland Regiment through much of the war's duration.

At the onset of the conflict in late summer 1914, Britain's Secretary of State for War, Lord Herbert Kitchener, veteran of the Sudan conflict and second Boer War and former Commander-in-Chief in India, was one of the few who foresaw a long battle. A much larger army would be needed than the small Professional Regular Army, and he organized the largest volunteer army ever assembled for Britain—in fact for the world. In Britain, these recruits were ordinary chaps—the same mix of students, shop assistants, and labourers found in any sample of the population of England, Scotland, Wales, and Ireland.[19] Their eagerness and resolve reflected the ideals of the Edwardian age,[20] soon to be eclipsed by so much more than time.

In the same way, any handful of Newfoundland Regiment

18 The Rooms, "Entering the Great War," *The Newfoundland Regiment and the Great War*, online, accessed June 2015.

19 W. David Parsons, "The Importance of Beaumont-Hamel," unpublished paper, submitted to the Centre for Newfoundland Archives, QE II Library, Memorial University, 2014.

20 Todman, *The Great War*, xi.

recruits could include bookkeepers, boilermakers, clerks, a chauffeur, bakers, coopers, sailmakers, and a salesman from the dry goods department of a Water Street shop.[21]

The start of the war was a time when groups of friends from sports teams or outdoor-enthusiast leagues or culture or business clubs enlisted together. These were known as the Pals Regiments or Pals Brigades.[22] Britain (like Newfoundland) had had no pre-war conscription, and a recruitment process that allowed men to join together with their friends, colleagues, and neighbours was very successful. Unfortunately, it would soon mean they died together, too, and some businesses and villages (and families and outports) would lose a whole generation of young men.[23]

In Germany, since 1871, every male between seventeen and forty-five was liable for military service. During peacetimes, the only requirement was registration. In more tumultuous periods, men were mustered and delegated for five years of service: three in the cavalry (few in the aristocratic command structure throughout the European armies strategized much beyond cavalry)[24] and two in other branches. Only those in prison were exempt. Germans who passed the required physicals and were deemed ready to fight were rated KV—*kriegsdienst verwendungsfahig*, fit for active service.[25]

On August 22, an enlistment proclamation appeared in the Newfoundland papers. Men between nineteen and thirty-five were sought to "serve abroad for the duration of the war, but not exceeding one year": privates would be paid $1.00 a day plus rations. There was a rush to become part of the great adventure before it was all over. As even the Kaiser

21 Major, personal interview.

22 Parsons, "The Importance of Beaumont-Hamel."

23 Neiberg, *Reader*, 10.

24 Todman, *The Great War*, xi.

25 Ferguson, *Pity of War*, xxxi.

told his troops, nobody expected the war to last until Christmas.[26]

That evening, the recruitment centre was opened in St. John's. On the first night, seventy-four men enlisted; within its first week, 275; in two weeks, 743, Robertson among them.

A training camp opened in Pleasantville. Government, businesses, and private citizens donated tents, and others were made from the sails of vessels in the harbour.

On October 3, the First Five Hundred, the Blue Puttees, which included Robertson, assigned to "A" Company of the 1st Battalion, marched from Pleasantville to the S.S. *Florizel*, a steamship sealer converted to troopship. They were cheered by a huge group of citizens.[27] "Red, white, and blue bunting draped many of the buildings and fluttered from the masts of ships anchored at the harbor. All business was suspended. Shortly before four o'clock, the Newfoundlanders fell in."[28]

Their first night aboard was actually spent in St. John's harbour. They were waiting to join a Canadian convoy for their Atlantic crossing. The next day, they sailed.

From the beginning, the Newfoundland Regiment enjoyed remarkable cohesion: "The Newfoundland Contingent possessed a unity which was without parallel. Probably at no time in history had so many men been recruited into a formed body of troops from such a relatively small area in so short a time, all sailing together and embarking from their own home port."[29]

On board, their training consisted of Company commanders

[26] Sweet, "Service Monday," A9.

[27] O'Neill, *The Oldest City*, 108.

[28] Colonel G.W.L. Nicholson, *The Fighting Newfoundlander: A History of The Royal Newfoundland Regiment* (Montreal: McGill-Queen's UP, 2006), 114.

[29] Ibid., 117-18.

lecturing their men for an hour each afternoon. There were religious services on the Sunday. One evening a concert was organized by Colour Sergeant Owen Steele, and a double quartette sang "My Bonnie Lies over the Ocean."[30]

The *Florizel* docked in Plymouth Sound, a bay in the English West Country, on October 14, the Newfoundland soldiers staying aboard until the 20th.

[30] Ibid., 119-20.

CHAPTER FOUR
A Proper Sport

OLYMPICS OR NO Olympics, athleticism itself was part of the militaristic ethos. In Germany, this philosophy was known as "Sport and Turnen" and was much encouraged by the army, at first in enthusiasm for the Olympic preparations, but continuing even as plans for the 1916 Olympics were shelved. Olympic idealism dovetailed with a search for a better way of training soldiers, and more efficient rehabilitation of their injuries.[31]

Even during the hostilities, sport continued as a regular part of life. Although in 1915 British competitive football was suspended for the duration, the soldiers played soccer from their trenches. It was a vital pastime, and taken quite seriously. Over 2,000 footballers had enlisted, sometimes as whole sides, and the numbers were enough to constitute special Football Battalions.[32] Leagues formed and competitions were held.[33]

Perhaps the most famous games were those of the 1914 Christmas truce, when soldiers of the British and German

31 Thierry Terret and J.A. Mangan eds, *Sport, Militarism and the Great War* (London: Routledge, 2012), 13.

32 John Simkin, "Football and The First World War," *Spartacus Educational*, online, accessed August 2015.

33 Terret and Mangan, *Sport*, 13.

trenches on the Western Front initiated an unofficial ceasefire that progressed from shaking hands, singing Christmas carols, and allowing time for religious services and burials, to exchanging gifts of chocolate, cigarettes, and schnapps—and playing football. In their letters home, soldiers described the events (which also included trading souvenirs and impromptu hairdressing) as "unique and weird," "absolutely astounding," and "marvelous."[34] (Shorter ad-hoc truces, allowing soldiers on both sides to eat, rescue wounded men, or simply pass a few peaceful hours without the barrage of artillery, were fairly common.[35] And, sometimes, enemy night patrols might take good care not to sight each other.)[36]

This was not the only time that sport spanned a gap between the two sides. In the prisoner-of-war camps, the German guards watched with interest as the English and French prisoners played soccer[37]; although, the camps, like everything else, were strained by pre-war thinking that the conflict would be swift and decisive. Even within that pre-supposed timeframe, the Germans were surprised by the numbers of soldiers they captured as the British Expeditionary Force

34 These truces incited the military establishment on both sides. They were thought to result from the soldiers' proximity, as the trenches were so close and the men kept there so long the two sides became familiar with each other through shouted conversations. Adolf Hitler, then a young German corporal, was particularly opposed to them. Participants in the Christmas truce could be severely punished, even court-martialed for treason, and on subsequent Christmas Eves, special bombardments were ordered to stifle any potential outbreaks of seasonal peaceful lulls. The news of this fraternization was embargoed and censored to various degrees by all the nations involved. On November 11, 2008, ancestors of those British and German soldiers restaged the Christmas Day match. The Germans won 2-1. There are many sources for information about the 1914 Christmas Truce, including, Malcolm Brown ed, *Meeting in No Man's Land: Christmas 1914 and Fraternization in the Great War*, (London: Constable, 2007).

35 Tony Ashworth, "The Live and Let Live Syndrome," in Neiberg, *Reader*, 208-211.

36 Ferguson, *Pity of War*, 343.

37 Terret and Mangan, *Sport*, 2-3.

retreated across the River Marne in late August and early September 1914.

Germany, like Britain and the other nations embroiled in the conflict, wanted to show it was treating its war prisoners well. Of course, the prisoner soldiers were also sources of enemy intelligence and could be used as hostages.[38] But official (and more reassuringly humane) photographs showing, for example, British soldiers giving German captors cigarettes and a drink were widely and officially publicized.[39] It was good propaganda (a term known in French as *bourrage de crane* or skull stuffing).[40] Propaganda was not necessarily a negative term at this time: it simply presented information through text and, especially, imagery, often appearing on that democratic form of communication—posters—as something emotional, something positive and evocative without necessarily being absolutely logical.[41]

With the existing facilities overwhelmed even before the war continued past Christmas 1914,[42] more camps needed to be built and organized, and the prisoners delegated for labour in mines or forestry and agriculture or factories. (Regular Sunday football matches would continue to be part of their routine.)

As the war lasted, conditions at the camps, on both sides, could vary from fairly decent to intolerable. Soldiers from every country endured them. Any embroiled nation could reference the signature news photograph of prisoners staring out through barbed wire. It happened to all of them. Indeed they had all of the WWI iconography in common: the

38 Ferguson, *Pity of War*, 371.

39 Ibid. 367.

40 Neiberg, *Reader*, 15.

41 Hadley and Legler, *Posters*, 13-14

42 Heather Jones, "Prisoners of War," *The British Library*, online, accessed September 2014.

trenches, the gas attacks, the stretcher-bearers foundering through the muck of No Man's Land.[43] In fact, WWI posters from every nation, whether championing recruitment, war bonds, or sheer patriotism, often featured similar if not identical iconography, especially the hero figure of the lone battle-weary but resolute soldier.[44]

These symbols also flickered into moving images. The first documentary of WWI—of any war—*The Battle of the Somme*, debuted in Britain on August 21, 1916. Its most famous sequences showed soldiers going over the top. That these were later considered staged, not true, footage, diluted none of their impact. They only reinforced the choreography the public believed the soldiers had followed by their orders and to their death on 1 July 1916.[45] (This was the film seen by the widest audience in Britain until *Star Wars* in 1977.)[46]

These classic examples of WWI propaganda were largely produced outside of official government agencies. Instead, they were filtered through popular culture and especially spooled through cinema (although the British War Office, for one, would sometimes commission a film).[47] German film companies, too, shot and screened titles like *How Max Won the Iron Cross*, and *Miss Field-Grey*. These helped fill the

43 "For here mud stands for much more than a mere amalgam of water and soil. It is made up of excrement, dead soldiers and animals, shrapnel, barbed wire and the remnants of poison gas. For all the opportunities it offered to bacteria, surrounding splintered trees and dead men, it seems to be opposed to nature. This mud bears the terrifying potential to engulf the soldiers who struggle through it, to suck them down–sputtering, choking, drowning–and to convert their corpses into yet more mud." Todman, *The Great War*, 1.

44 Frederick Hadley and Martin Legler, *Posters of the Great War* (South Yorkshire: Pen & Sword Military, 2013), 63.

45 Ian F. Beckett, *The Making of the First World War* (New Haven: Yale UP, 2012), 87-8.

46 Hadley and Legler, *Posters*, 129.

47 Ferguson, *Pity of War*, 226.

void created by the banning of all foreign films.[48] And along with academic manifestos, bellicose poetry, and flag-waving editorials, companies in many nations produced war-inspired toys and comics including tanks, pea-firing artillery, and "In France, *Lusitania* jigsaws and a militarized version of Monopoly."[49]

A nation's mentality was compressed into these cultural touchstones. As mentioned, propaganda was not automatically stamped as negative. It was a discussion between nations, or between a nation and itself, and the values of courage, determination, or heroism were shared by all involved, like the lonely stalwart soldier who was so often the central image on British, French, and German posters.[50] Even a soldier who was hurt or injured, bearing a sling, crutch, or bandages, stayed brave and determined. The enemy was neither, and often dehumanized, depicted on German posters, for example, as a dragon, fought and felled by Siegfried.[51] In the eyes of the Allies, Germany could be distilled into the image of a spiked helmet.[52]

Yet, along with this celebration of militarism, these countries also increasingly shared the sense that these soldiers formed a generation being lost in vain. No huge gains were being made by any side. Eventually, The War to End All Wars arguably prevented none, while "The greater destruction of the Second World War contributes to an understandable yet misleading image of the First as a senseless waste, the ultimate expression of a wrong war fought for the wrong reasons."[53] No one, not even the soldiers, saw the point of it, its genesis lost in a fog of whispers:

48 Ferguson, *Pity of War*, 227.

49 Ibid., 229

50 Hadley and Legler, *Posters*, 63.

51 Ibid., 81.

52 Ibid., 97.

53 Neiberg, *Reader*, 3.

> Baldrick: I heard it started when some chap called Archie Duke shot an ostrich because he was hungry.
> Blackadder: I think you mean it started when the Arch-Duke of Austro-Hungary got shot.
> Baldrick: No–there was definitely an ostrich involved.
> Blackadder: Well, possibly. But the real reason for the whole thing was that it was just too much effort not to have a war.[54]

In post-war memoirs, both soldiers and politicians often compare the war's origins and onslaught to natural forces—typhoons, plagues, the irresistible pull of planetary orbits.[55] In hindsight, it was viewed as profoundly inevitable. Others later reviewed the military and political planning for conflict and concluded that these policies and preparations constructed such an unwieldly stack they toppled into war on their own.[56] But no one could point to a necessary incitement, a worthwhile gain: "The futility of combat in the First World War stands out as perhaps its single most defining characteristic."[57]

Analysis of this found myriad contributing factors. The technical problems included fatal weakness in military command and communications. At the outbreak of war the British Expeditionary Force had no effective methods for air observation, aerial photography, or signals communication. They didn't even have proper maps.

> Communication networks stopped at the front line, so that as soon as troops left that point their position was unknown. During battle, despite elaborate precautions such as burying cable in triplicate along different

[54] Todman, *The Great War*, 145; Richard Curtis. *Blackadder: The Whole Damn Dynasty, 1485-1917*, (London: Penguin, 1980) 412.

[55] Ferguson, *Pity of War*, xxxv.

[56] Ibid., xxxvii.

[57] Neiberg, *Reader*, 13.

> routes, communications were more than likely to be cut off by enemy shellfire. Generals therefore had to rely on fragmentary reports from runners. It was not until 1918 that armies developed sophisticated signals services and had access to wireless sets. This flaw in communications technology cannot be overestimated as an explanation for high casualties on the attacking side. As [Richard] Holmes has put it, "it was not primarily the growth of killing power that gave the Western Front its distinctive character: it was the fact that communications always lagged behind weaponry. It was always easier for a defender, driven back on his own communications, to reinforce his failure than it was for an attacker, his communication stretched across the abrasive edge of the battlefield, to reinforce his success.[58]

Added to this, "The entire culture of the British regular army militated against effective improvisation."[59] This despite the huge numbers of soldiers involved. The total mobilization figures for the combatants were Britain, 8.4 million; France, 7.9 million; Germany, 13.2 million; Russia, 15.8 million; USA, 4.3 million.[60]

Perhaps its sheer human mass allowed the fighting to somehow develop a life, and a timeline, of its own. Even contemporary advertising picked up on this perplexity, such as this text, placed by a Canadian laundromat:

> How Long Will the War Last?
>
> The whole world is asking this question. Lord Kitchener intimates it may last three years. Kaiser Bill told his soldiers they would be back in Germany before the leaves begin to fall…

58 Ferguson, *Pity of War*, 304.

59 Ibid., 305.

60 Ibid., xxiv.

> Meanwhile economical living is being practiced, and thousands are benefiting through the saving which is possible by the Dry Cleaning process.
>
> –advertisement by a Halifax laundry, November 13, 1914[61]

Not only was the war supposed to be over by Christmas, but to one young German lieutenant, "War is like Christmas." All involved nations had entered the fray fueled by the enthusiasm of thousands and thousands of young men.[62] A Berlin journalist wrote, "We lack the words to describe these experiences…We are standing in the middle of the greatest joys of our lives. Our victory wagon[63] has departed and will no longer be able to be held back."[64]

But Christmas came and passed and 1914 became 1915. The short, decisive combat European powers had been building up to for four decades was over, "but nobody had won it."[65]

The Newfoundland Regiment had spent those early months training in Edinburgh, Stob's Camp, and Ayr. Robertson's conduct was noted as fairly good: four instances of being late or absent from parade, each earning him two or three days of being confined to base. On September 1, they were sent to Alexandria, and on the 13th, Gallipoli. Robertson endured a month there before illness saw him transferred to the hospital ship *Valdivia*, then to a hospital in Mudros. From there he was brought via Port Suez and Marseilles to England. He would rejoin the Regiment in France.

61 Nicholson, *Fighting Newfoundlander*, 195.

62 Jeffrey Verhey, "Soldiers, War Enthusiasm: Volunteers, Departing Soldiers, and Victory Celebrations," in Neiberg, *Reader*, 159.

63 Also in keeping with military tactics of the time, the victory wagon was horse-drawn. All the nation's armies relied on horses, and 8 million horses and mules perished during the war. Neiberg, *Reader*, 195.

64 Neiberg, *Reader*, 155.

65 Michael Howard, *The First World War: A Very Short Introduction* (London: Oxford UP, 2002), 36.

CHAPTER FIVE
Z Day

"Heard we are to go to France in April."
– Lieutenant-Colonel Arthur Lovell Hadow, appointed officer commanding the 1st Battalion, Newfoundland Regiment, December 6, 1915, while the Regiment was serving in Gallipoli. Personal diary, mid-January, 1914.[66]

Z-DAY, THE START of the Big Push, was originally scheduled for June 29, but postponed due to weather. It was envisioned as a systematic progression of firepower from guns and howitzers and mortars against the German trenches and observation and machine-gun posts building into a continuous and lethal cascade.[67] The German retreat would be rapid, the British victory decisive. This would bring an end to the war.

This contemporary account describes the lead up to the battle:

> The scene of the battlefields at night was of terrible beauty…The fields at the edge of the battle of guns were very peaceful…A staff officer had whispered a secret to us at midnight in a little room, when the door was shut and the window closed. Even then they were words which could only be whispered, and to men of trust… The attack will be made this morning at 7:30.

66 Nicholson, *Fighting Newfoundlander*, 232.
67 Nicholson, *Fighting Newfoundlander*, 253-61.

> It was 7:30. Our watches told us that, but nothing else. The guns had lifted and were firing behind the enemy's first lines, but there was no sudden hush for the moment of attack. The barrage by our guns seemed as great as the first bombardment. For ten minutes or so before this time a new sound had come into the general thunder of artillery. It was like the "rafale" of the French soixante-quinze, very rapid, with distant and separate strokes, but louder than the noise of field-guns. They were our trench-mortars at work, along the whole length of the line before me.
>
> It was 7:30. The moment for the attack had come. Clouds of smoke had been liberated to form a screen for the infantry, and hid the whole line. The only men I could see were those in reserve, winding along a road by some trees which led up to the attacking point. They had their backs turned, as they marched very slowly and steadily forward. I could not tell who they were, though I had passed some of them on the road a day or two before. But, whoever they were, English, or Irish, or Welsh, I watched them until most had disappeared from sight behind a clump of trees. In a little while they would be fighting, and would need all their courage.
>
> At a minute after 7:30 there came through the rolling smoke-clouds a rushing sound. It was the noise of rifle fire and machine-guns. The men were out of their trenches, and the attack had begun.[68]

Soon after, Hadow, as the Newfoundland Regiment's Battalion Commander, sent for information, asking, "Has the enemy's front line been captured?" But the response was not encouraging: "The situation is not cleared up."[69]

[68] Philip Gubbs, "The Historic First of July," in Neiberg, *Reader*, 185-190.

[69] Nicholson, *Fighting Newfoundlander*, 269.

The Regiment had started from St. John's Road, crossing about 250 yards of ground, under enemy fire, before they reached even their own front line. When "A" Company and "B" Company struggled their way through their front wire, they could look down the incline and observe the barrier of German wire. It was supposed to be cut to pieces. It was not.

Still, the Regiment continued its advance. They were alone and exposed to the full brunt of enemy fire.

Within a half hour, Hadow made his way to Brigade Battle Headquarters, where he reported to Brigadier-General Douglas Edward Cayley that the attack had failed and the Regiment's casualties were high. Regardless, Cayley ordered Hadow to assemble whatever remnants of the Regiment he could find and attempt another advance. Fortunately, this order was soon countermanded; in any case, Hadow could not find a single uninjured one of his soldiers.[70] Robertson was among the wounded; in fact, his fate at that exact time may have been unknown, as he had gone over the top, been shot in his right leg, and was now lying wounded in the field.

Field Marshall Douglas Haig had deployed 120,000 men that morning. Because he was assured in his assumption that the preceding wire cutting and barrages had succeeded in erasing enemy defences, many of his soldiers were not fitted out for attack, but carting equipment to fortify positions supposed to have been secured by the artillery.

Instead, more than 19,000 British soldiers died and 14,000 were wounded—to this day the worst losses in the history of the British army. Altogether, The Somme, as the 1916 battle was then known, would prove the most disastrous engagement of the First World War. In less than five months, there were more than a million casualties: 420,000 for the

70 Nicholson, *Fighting Newfoundlander*, 270-2.

British, 420,000 for the Germans, and 200,000 for the French.

The ground itself would be contested again and again until the Armistice in 1918. By then, soldiers from more than twenty-five countries had fought there, "Perhaps making it the place that best describes the World War. Americans, Australians, Canadian, Chinese, Indians, Irishmen, Moroccans, New Zealanders, Senegalese, South Africans...had all come to the Somme."[71]

Without victory, the losses encapsulated what could be called "a folk memory,"[72] "the British group-memory, the epitome of incompetent generalship and pointless sacrifice"[73] that resonated for decades.

From *Blackadder Goes Forth*:

> Melchett: Now, Field Marshal Haig has formulated a brilliant tactical plan to ensure final victory in the field.
>
> Blackadder: Would this brilliant plan involve us climbing over the top of our trenches and walking slowly towards the enemy?
>
> Darling: How did you know that Blackadder? It's classified information.
>
> Blackadder: It's the same plan we used the last time sir. And the seventeen times before that.
>
> *They all move over to the desk.*
>
> Melchett: E-e-exactly! And that's what's so brilliant about it. It will catch the watchful Hun totally off guard. Doing exactly what we've done eighteen times before will be the last thing they expect us to do this time. There is, however, one problem.

[71] Hadley and Legler, *Posters*, 6.

[72] Ferguson, *Pity of War*, xxxii.

[73] Howard, *The First World War*, 65.

> Blackadder: That everyone always gets slaughtered in the first ten seconds?
>
> Melchett: Exactly. Field Marshal Haig is concerned that this may be depressing the men a tadge, so he's looking for a way to cheer the men up.
>
> Blackadder: His resignation and suicide seem the obvious answer.[74]

When the war was over, Newfoundland's Commission of Government negotiated with over 200 French landowners to purchase and preserve sixteen hectares of land at Beaumont-Hamel. Newfoundland seedlings—including spruce, fir, dogberry, and juniper—were shipped over and planted.[75] Visitors arrived to pay their respects almost as soon as the war ended.[76]

74 Todman, *The Great War*, 116; *Blackadder:The Whole Damn Dynasty*, 354.

75 Kevin Major, *No Man's Land: A Play*, (St. John's: Pennywell Books, 2005) 10.

76 Ferguson, *Pity of War*, xxxx; Ferguson also notes that, in *Tender is the Night*, F. Scott Fitzgerald's Dick Driver visits the trenches six years after the war. His party was particularly moved by the fate of the Newfoundlanders.

CHAPTER SIX

Nothing but the End of the World

ALTHOUGH INVALIDED AWAY from the Front, and convalescing in Wandsworth in London, Robertson was still not shielded entirely from the remainder of the war. The country now operated under the Defence of the Realm Act. The war would bring rationing and blackouts. The capital cities of Britain, Germany, and France all became settings for the theatre of war. Paris, for example, was bombed in 1914—almost 700,000 civilians left Paris in September of that year[77]—and shelled in 1918.[78]

London in 1914 was a city of youth: "Fully 38 per cent under the age of twenty in 1911." Most Londoners had been born there, and their sense of identity was forged in their particular and distinct boroughs: Croydon, Islington, Chelsea, Hackney, Greenwich, Lambeth, Kensington, Westminster.[79] Together they comprised a major global power in itself, the "financial capital of the world."[80]

London appeared to have braced itself for the conflict, even embraced it. For many months before August 1914, the city, and the country, expected war, and their expectations were

77 Ferguson, *Pity of War*, 186.

78 Hadley and Legler, *Posters*, 113.

79 Jay Winter and Jean-Louis Robert eds, *Capital Cities at War: Paris, London, Berlin 1914-1918* (Cambridge: Cambridge UP, 1997), 30.

80 Ibid., 32.

often steeped in enthusiasm. This was reflected in, and perhaps partly generated by, the popular fiction of the day (for example, L. James's *The Boy Galloper*, William Le Queux's serialized bestseller *The Invasion of 1910*, or Walter Woods's *The Enemy in Our Midst*).[81] Conspiracies of German spy rings were a popular motif, although curiously, and presciently, many books did not posit a war with the Germans, but a conflagration ignited by an assassination in the Balkans.[82] Others cast Russia or even France as the more natural British enemy. P.G. Wodehouse went even further (of course) in *The Swoop!, or, How Clarence Saved England: A Tale of Great Invasion*, published in 1909, which saw its hero defend his nation from attack (on the August Bank Holiday, no less) by Germany, Russia, Switzerland, China, Monaco, and Morocco.[83]

Such frivolity flirted with being considered anti-militarist, not patriotic. And there were some who did openly express such controversial viewpoints: those who looked back on the Boer Wars (1880-1881, 1889-1902, pitting the United Kingdom against the South African Republic and the Orange State) as disastrous foreign policy; labour organizers who saw only peacetime as potential for radical, trans-national union and work improvements; and those beginning to follow the new philosophy of pacifism. But once war was declared, an author like H.G. Wells was not alone in rushing to demonize the enemy; Wells even had a powerful image ready in his forward-thinking mind, a gigantic lethal machine: unwieldly, unearthly, its twister body with tentacled arms of havoc continuously stoking its maw's appetite for total war.[84]

Indeed, the declaration of war was celebrated in the streets all over Britain. (In Germany the pubic fervour was known

81 Ferguson, *Pity of War*, 1-2.

82 Ibid., 4.-5

83 Ibid., 6.

84 Ibid., 233.

as *erhebung*, "exaltation").[85] The British government called for 100,000 volunteers; 750,000 signed up within a month. Conscientious objectors—a new term—were reviled and any seeming able-bodied man not in uniform could be shamed with a white feather or refused service in shops and pubs. This public attitude was somewhat checked by the Battle of the Marne, September 5th to the 12th,1914; although the Germans were defeated while fighting on two fronts, casualties and losses were high all around, and neither side clenched the decisive victory it had felt was within its grasp.[86] The Battle of the Marne also drove the anticipated short war into the stalemate of the trenches.

Civilians absorbed these shifts and setbacks, just as they had adjusted to the first huge mobilizations of volunteer soldiers, and then the many of those who were lost or maimed. They were firmly behind the soldiers: what those men suffered, they at home would also bear.[87] And the dangers were shared. While the German U-boats, for example, could not physically attack people on land, their strategies produced food shortages, and prices rose.[88] And the German Navy conducted coastal raids on Britain, including one against Scarborough, Whitby, and Hartlepool that killed 199 on December 16, 1914. Zeppelin raids began May 31, 1915; fifty more followed.[89] Aerial and artillery bombardment would kill over 1,000 civilians in London and Paris, and, before the war ended, 1,500 across Britain.[90]

An eyewitness described an air raid on London on 13 June 1917, originally planned for twenty German aircraft:

[85] Ibid., 175.

[86] Chris Trueman, "The Home Front 1914 to 1918," *The History Learning Site*, online, accessed July 2014.

[87] Winter and Robert eds, *Capital Cities*, 14.

[88] Trueman, "The Home Front."

[89] Ibid.

[90] Ibid.

> But two turned back with engine trouble and a third did so after dropping its bombs on Margate...Three more broke away once over the English coast...The remaining 14, flying in a rough diamond formation, appeared at about 15,000 feet over London at about 1130 hours in bright sunshine.
>
> Many people on the ground assumed they were British aircraft and took no cover. The attack was centred on Liverpool Street Station. An American journalist [Ian Castle] on a bus noted that 'men and women strangely stood still, gazing up into the air. The conductor mounted the stairs to suggest that outside passengers should seek safety inside. Some of them did so. 'I'm not a religious man,' remarked the conductor, 'but what I say is, we are all in God's hands and if we are going to die we may as well die quiet.' But some inside passengers were determined that if they had to die quiet they might as well see something first and they climbed on top and with wonderstruck eyes watched the amazing drama of the skies.[91]

Civilians were also killed in ammunition factory accidents. The worst was an explosion in Silverton, in London's East End, January 19, 1917, with sixty-nine dead and over 400 injured.[92]

As the fighting continued, civilians learned their war news through the press (and both British and French newspapers were fined and suspended for reporting such stories as the unhygienic conditions of transports of wounded soldiers. It was not just military news that could get them into trouble either, but also political thought deemed counterproductive to the war effort).[93] Letters from the front could also be

[91] Beckett, *The Making of the First World War*, 170-1.

[92] Trueman, "The Home Front."

[93] Ferguson, *Pity of War*, 220-221.

censored, often by the soldiers themselves, not wanting to distress their friends and family. Trainloads of wounded soldiers were timed to arrive late at night, out of public sight and acknowledgement. But there was no hiding that there was much to fear and mourn. The home front had its own terrible terrors and attritions. As one English woman, Vera Brittain, wrote to her fiancé, Roland Leighton,

> Oxford 7 May 1915
>
> It is horrible to think of you under shell fire, & in support trenches. I suppose you really are very near the vast chaos that was Ypres—if not actually in it. I wonder, if all this ever ends—sometimes I feel as if nothing but the end of the world could finish it—& you are still left to us, if you will be very different. I supposed you are bound to be—people, especially those who[se] sensibilities are fine and keen, can't go through this sort of thing & remain the same.[94]

But Leighton was not left to them. He died December 23, 1915, just as he was expected home for Christmas,[95] and Vera would later write her brother Edward:

> 1st London General, 28 June 1916
>
> I believe I heard the guns here a day or two ago. What a clamour must be going on! One anxiety is more than enough; & sometimes I feel quite glad that Roland is lying where the guns cannot disturb Him however loudly they are & He cannot any more hear the noise they make.[96]

94 Vera Brittain, "Letters from a Lost Generation," in Neiberg, *Reader*, 233.

95 Brittain, "Return of a Dead Officer's Kit," *The Guardian*, online, last updated 14 November 2008.

96 Brittain, "Letters," 238. Vera Brittain (1893-1970) volunteered as a VAD during WWI and was later a writer best known for her memoir *Testament of Youth* (1930). Besides Roland and Edward, she also lost two very good friends during the war.

Edward, too, would fall. The personal cost paid by many British families and individuals was very high. 1916 was a particularly terrible year; even income tax was raised, to twenty-five percent. At the same time, German civilians suffered as much or more. Not just in terms of casualties and shortages and rationing, but even in wage losses, as capital income dropped twenty-four percent, even as it rose in Britain.[97]

So even a soldier such as Robertson, rescued from the battlefield and convalescing in England, on the home front, would not have been immune to the culture shock and collateral damage of all-out war.

93 Ferguson, *Pity of War*, 276.

CHAPTER SEVEN

A Soldier's Heart

EVEN IN MASSIVE conflicts like the American Civil War (1861-1865), with almost 650,000 casualties, it was disease, not enemy fire, that was the soldier's insidious enemy. In the nineteenth century, cholera or typhus felled more men than swords or shells. As with all forms of weaponry, WWI created new such foes for the soldiers: trench foot, trench fever, gas poisoning. But the illness that spread most rampantly was shellshock.

Although "since the Greco-Persian wars there had been accounts of men behaving abnormally in combat,"[98] in the First World War these incidents increased exponentially and created real manpower problems. They also affected outcomes on the battlefields, as soldiers on the front lines were reported, "running panic-stricken, casting away arms and equipment."[99]

Military commanders were unsure which soldiers were truly shell-shocked and which were too frightened or unwilling to fight. Diagnosing the genuine sufferer from the malingerer fell to doctors.

[98] Terry Copp and Mark Osborne Humphries, *Combat Stress in the 20th Century: The Commonwealth Perspective* (Kingston: Canadian Defence Academy Press, 2010), 1.

[99] David Rowland, *The Stress of Battle: Quantifying Human Performance in Combat* (London: TSO, 2006), 181.

Shellshock, though not always known by that term, had been studied for some time. Medical literature on the condition dated from the early seventeenth century, when it was called "nostalgia";[100] the soldiers lost all interest in the fighting and wanted only to return home. Their only relief seemed to be talking of home and family, but this was a reprieve, not a cure (which proved elusive). Even worse, from a general's point of view, one soldier's longing could infect another, which could prove epidemic to a force or fatal to an individual.[101]

Published reports of shellshock (or, as it was known in Britain, a "soldier's heart"[102]) appeared before the end of 1914 and "during the course of the conflict more than 120,000 British soldiers were pensioned off" with it.[103] The symptoms included shakiness, fatigue, terrible dreams; some sufferers went blind or deaf or mute.[104] The number of cases increased dramatically after July 1, 1916.[105]

Even as medical research progressed, many practitioners, as well as the military chain of command, felt the problem was sheer weakness of character—or worse, lack of courage. Hundreds of soldiers were shot for cowardice and desertion—Haig insisted on this punishment, fearing pardons would seriously dilute the morale and fighting strength of his forces.[106] (This judgement stood until 2006 when the families of the WWI soldiers so sentenced were told their executed relatives would receive posthumous pardons.)[107]

[100] Hadley and Legler, *Posters*, 63.

[101] Copp and Humphries, *Combat Stress*, 1 & 3.

[102] Copp and Humphries, *Combat Stress*, 2. In WWII it was called "battle fatigue," and is now known as "PTSD" or "Post-traumatic stress disorder," and it remains stigmatized. Gayle MacDonald, "A Picture of PTSD," *The Globe and Mail* (9 June 2014), L1.

[103] Copp and Humphries, *Combat Stress*, 8.

[104] Ibid., 9-10.

[105] Ibid., 11.

[106] Ferguson, *Pity of War*, 347.

[107] MacDonald, "PTSD," L1.

German evidence, too, suggested a soldier's personality, combined with his position in the field (for example whether he was near or on the front line), would determine whether he would develop a war neurosis. It was argued that soldiers away from the front, including prisoners of war, rarely displayed such an indisposition. And while the German soldiers might not be shot for desertion, the prescribed treatments could be terrible. After the war, German veterans cited Viennese psychiatric professor Julius Wagner-Jauregg for "the brutal use of electric-shock therapy to treat German soldiers invalided with functional somatic symptoms."[108]

Sigmund Freud, the Austrian neurologist and father of psychoanalysis, thought the problem affected only unwounded soldiers, as soldiers who were injured had a physical manifestation of their ordeal, but this was not borne out by the evidence and experience of the men who came through the war.

Similarly, the once-accepted thesis that prisoners of war could not be affected by battle trauma would also be dismissed, and by 1945 it was noted that prisoners of war often had more trouble than other soldiers re-adapting to civilian life. But during and after WWI this line of thought still prevailed, and was the accepted view of the War Congress of the German Psychiatric Association in Munich in September 1916.[109]

Still in the trenches, many soldiers steeped in their own trauma. They began to believe the war would simply never end.[110] They did not discuss this. Even after the war, the soldiers seldom talked about it, their experiences and their trauma.

Robertson rarely did.

108 Copp and Humphries, *Combat Stress*, 412.

109 Copp and Humphries, *Combat Stress*, 412.

110 Ferguson, *Pity of War*, 365.

CHAPTER EIGHT

More and More Beds

ROBERTSON WAS ADMITTED to the 3rd London General Hospital in the London suburb of Wandsworth on July 8, 1916. The institution had been automatically transformed from the Royal Patriotic School (formerly Asylum) to a War Hospital on August 5, 1914, the day after war was declared. The building dated from 1859, established for the orphaned daughters of soldiers and sailors who had fought in the Crimean War (1854-1856). These children were allotted to nearby homes for the duration of this new conflict.

There were four Territorial General Hospitals in London, and the 3rd was the one in need of the most alterations:

> The metamorphosis of the school into the hospital was an extremely complicated task: not only had practically all the school's furniture to be removed, but many structural changes were made: the windows altered, hopper sashes put in, lavatories and baths attached to those rooms which were to become wards, and so forth.[111]

The dining room became the reception ward. The entrance hall housed the telephone exchange. Lifts were installed and the kitchen expanded. A bronze statue of Kitchener was on prominent display.

111 "The Origin of the 3rd L.G.H…Reprinted from The Gazette of the 3rd London General Hospital, February 1917," *The WWI Document Archive*, online, accessed July 2014.

The main building was now composed of wards for medical and surgical cases, with two large wards for ophthalmic patients, whose eyes had been injured by gas. For patients deemed insane, there was the standard specially designed environment, a padded room.

The influx of shellshocked soldiers continued. By May 1915, all four Territorial General Hospitals had been required to establish neurological sections for patients suffering shellshock, also termed neurasthenia—fatigue, anxiety, headaches, neuralgia, and depression.

An X-ray department was much in use for detecting any bullets that remained inside soldiers. A camp for infectious diseases was isolated from the main structure. There was a mortuary and a post-mortem room and three chapels, one adorned with an ivory crucifix, a personal gift from Queen Amelie of Portugal.

To facilitate the transportation of wounded, who were being brought from their landings on England's south coast, a temporary railway station was built out front.

Almost immediately it was obvious the facility, with 200 beds, was too small. Ten hutted wards holding twenty or twenty-five beds, of corrugated iron covered in asbestos felt and featuring a verandah (dubbed "Bungalow Town"), and an operating theatre, were ordered and constructed in eight weeks, allowing for 520 beds. Even then, the expansions continued. By May 1916, the 3rd in Wandsworth had 2000 beds. Altogether it became one of the largest hospitals in Britain. It was also the first to use women from the Voluntary Aid Detachment instead of male soldiers—a controversial but ultimately effective and widely adopted move.

The 3rd had its own special division. Several patients had severe facial injuries and sculptor Francis Derwent Wood, who was too old to enlist and volunteered at the hospital instead, offered to help them. The War Office accepted his aid and Wood set up the Masks for Facial Disfigurement Department (aka the "tin noses shop"). He took facial casts and made prosthetic masks of silvered copper, which were painted to match skin tone and held in place with spectacles. These innovative artworks allowed acutely scarred soldiers an entry back into the world, a face that could be shown in public.

In fact, the 3rd benefited from the talents of many other artists, writers, and sculptors from the Chelsea Arts Club who were too old for service and volunteered as orderlies. For example, they also produced a monthly magazine, *The Gazette*. All the hospitals had such publications, but *The Gazette* was one of the finest.

This contributed to the 3rd's excellent reputation for treatment. By November 1917, 40,000 patients had been admitted, and only 270 died. By the time it closed in August 1920, over 62,708 patients from throughout the British Empire had been admitted to the hospital.

The building then became an orphanage once more, until 1938 when the children were evacuated to Hertfordshire with the threat of another world war. The children never returned to London.[112]

As Robertson continued to recover,[113] he spent time in London and Oxford and on assignment with the Regimental Depot in Ayr. He was discharged August 28, 1917, as medically

112 "The Origin of the 3rd L.G.H.," *World War I Document Archive*, online, accessed July 2014. During WWII, M16, the branch dedicated to foreign intelligence, used the building for detention and interrogation. It later became run-down, abandoned, and a target for vandals. In the 1980s it was sold for one pound sterling, and was renovated and repurposed. The structure still stands and now includes apartments, artists' studios, a drama school, and a French restaurant.

113 While Robertson was in hospital, a "Mr. Roy M. Robertson" received permission to visit him; the pass refers to Robertson as Eric's "brother," but Roy Robertson was more likely a cousin.

unfit, returned to St. John's, and went back to work with his father. The war would officially end on the Western Front at 11 am, November 11, 1918.

About one in eight of the men who fought, died.[114] Yet no country could point to substantial gains; in fact, entire empires—German, Russian, Turkish, and Austrian—were vastly diminished or entirely effaced. Nations were fractured into new states like Yugoslavia. France reclaimed the territories of Alsace and Lorraine, lost to the German Empire in 1871. France and Britain also gained the Middle Eastern "mandates" of Syria, Iraq, Lebanon, Iraq, and Palestine, where Britain was committed to establishing a Jewish national home. While America stood on the brink of its financial and military superpower, almost all "The victors of the First World War had paid a price far in excess of the value of all their gains; a price so high, indeed, that they would very shortly find themselves quite unable to hold on to most of them."[115]

[114] Hadley and Legler, *Posters*, 141.
[115] Ferguson, *Pity of War*, 434-436.

CHAPTER NINE

A Very Game Race

ON MARCH 13, 1919, Robertson was awarded the 1914-15 Star General Service and Victory Medals, which were given to those who had served in Gallipoli, Mudros, Lomnos, or the Western Egyptian Frontier. Regular medical examinations had found his wounds "soundly healed." But his leg still troubled him.

That same year, he returned to London to apprentice and liaison with Fortnum & Harvey, a landmark establishment and one of his father's company's clients. As part of his recuperation, Robertson joined the Polytechnic Harriers running club in London. As at school, he was running for his own reasons, to strengthen his leg, not to be ranked or win prizes. But at some point he did set a competitive goal for himself: to run the marathon in the first post-WWI Olympics.[116]

The word *marathon* came into English-language usage in the late nineteenth century, defining a footrace run on a set

[116] One Newfoundland-born athlete had already competed in the Olympics: Robert Fowler, who ran with the American track and field team in 1904 in St. Louis. And in 1924, Newfoundland-born Harry "Moose" Watson would score the gold-medal-winning goal for the Canadian team at the Winter Olympics in Chamonix, France. But both these sportsmen, though Newfoundlanders by birth, had left the island very young and were members of other national teams. Only Robertson arrived at an Olympics representing the independent nation of Newfoundland.

course measuring twenty-six miles and 385 yards, or 42.195 kilometres. The word comes from a village in Greece associated with a significant battle of 490 BC, when the Athenians, though outnumbered, triumphed over the Persian Empire.[117]

When the Olympics were reinstated in Athens in 1896, a marathon was structured from the Marathon battlefield to the Panathenaikon Stadium, rebuilt for the Games. It was a new addition to the lineup: the ancient Games did not have marathons, or any long-distance running, but instead featured *stades*, a stadium-length sprint, or *dolichos*, composed of 24 *stades*.[118]

But in the later nineteenth century, long-distance walking and running had become very fashionable in Britain and America with amateur distance racing and track-and-field events at schools and universities. Public contests were popular, and men placed bets on the distance one could cover by walking or run-walking for an hour, day, or week. This interest coalesced into a new sport called "pedestrianism."[119]

The activity, and its avowedly amateur adherents, meshed nicely with the ideals of the re-booted Games. Among other philosophies, de Coubertin sought a way to imbue social values through sport, to increase cohesion among athletes who practiced different sports, and to cleanse sport of commercialism and monetary goals (especially from athletes paid to lose).[120]

There weren't even gold medals at the first marathon; only the top two athletes received medals, and they were silver and bronze.[121] (Some athletes were also awarded prizes of

117 David E. Martin and Roger W.H. Gynn, *The Olympic Marathon* (Champaign, IL: Human Kinetics, 2000), 1.

118 Martin and Gynn, *Marathon*, 3.

119 Ibid., 3-4.

120 Ibid., 4-5.

121 Ibid., 20.

porcelain pottery.) The 1904 Games introduced the practice of awarding medals to the top three athletes.[122] This was now the ceremony of the post-WWI Olympics, held in the summer of 1920, in Antwerp.

Belgium was awarded the seventh Olympiad at an IOC meeting in Lausanne, Switzerland, in April 1919. It was a political and moral gesture towards Belgium's suffering during WWI. Antwerp itself was almost in ruins with much of its transportation infrastructure razed.[123] This in turn affected the Games, which were remarkable for their poor standard of facilities (the running track in particular was pitted and rutted), awful weather, low attendance (few could afford the tickets, and the stands were eventually filled with schoolchildren who received free entry), and deficit (626 million Belgian francs).[124]

But they were held, and they boasted a record-breaking roster of 2,607 athletes. The 1920 Olympics also (at last) debuted de Coubertin's Olympic flag of five rings, the colours of blue, yellow, white, red, and black representational of all the flags of all the nations, against a white field representing peace,[125] first created and displayed in 1914 (de Coubertin had also created the Olympic motto, *Citius*, *Altius*, *Fortius*: Faster, Higher, Stronger, which would be formally adopted in 1924).

As host country, Belgium issued the invitations. Its former enemy nations—Germany, Hungary, Austria, Bulgaria, and Turkey—did not receive one. There was no dedicated athletes' village; instead, the contestants were boarded throughout Antwerp, mostly in schools, sleeping on hard cots

122 Ibid., 36.

123 Miller, *The Official History*, 73.

124 John R. Gold, *Olympic Cites: City Agendas, Planning and the World's Games* (London: Routledge, 2007), 27.

125 Miller, *The Official History*, 72.

with hay-filled pillows, excepting for a time the Americans, first confined to their transport ship, the last minute replacement USS *Princess Matoika* (a referent name for Pocahontas), until their protests over its inadequate facilities reached mutinous heights. They were delivered to their appropriate sport venues in open trucks, "cheered on by townspeople." The program included aquatics, boxing, fencing, wrestling, polo, and the last appearance of tug of war (Great Britain won). Participants included 2,591 male and seventy-eight female athletes from twenty-nine countries, with New Zealand, Argentina, and Brazil participating for the first time as autonomous teams. A newly independent Finland, too, was competing under its own flag.[126]

Finland's most acclaimed athlete was its returning long-distance champion, Hannes Kolehmainen. The genial "Smiling Hannes" was the first of the great Olympic distance runners and the first of the Flying Finns, the generation of Finnish long-distance runners who would come to dominate the sport for the next several Olympiads. The next rising star, Paavo Nurmi, who ran at a precisely timed mechanical pace, was just beginning his ascendency. Together he and Kolehmainen would help Finland earn an astonishing nine gold medals in track and field in 1920—equal to mighty America.

Kolehmainen himself had won three gold medals in 1912 in Stockholm. But he was modest in his victory, known for his gentleman's attitude of humility towards his successes and generosity towards his competitors.

But, at Antwerp, if he looked for his contemporary rivals he would find only ghosts. In 1912, Jean Bouin of France had lost the 5000m to Kolehmainen by just 0.1 second, less than

[126] Miller, *The Official History*, 73-74. The newly formed Soviet Union, though, refused to engage in such a bourgeois affair; they would not enter the Olympics until 1952.

half a metre in one of the most exciting Olympic races in history. George Hutson of Britain was almost as strong a challenger, winning two bronze medals.[127] But they were not at the starting line in Antwerp. Bouin had died early in the war, on September 29, 1914, aged twenty-five; Hutson at twenty-four was even younger and had died even earlier, on September 14, in the Battle of the Marne. Hutson's body was never recovered, testament that heavy artillery had proven equal to the task of completely erasing the human body.

It was a large field, with forty-eight athletes running. Seventeen nations were represented by bib number, but, because of Robertson, eighteen by citizenship. Most of the marathoners had qualified by racing in their home country, or using times from an official race in another country where they happened to be living at the time. They came from eleven European nations, Canada and the US, Japan, India, and a single entry from each of South Africa, Australia, and Chile.

Newfoundland was never a member of the IOC. It had no Olympic committee or equivalent national sports body to confirm Robertson's amateur status and qualifications. He had simply and intrepidly travelled to Antwerp on his own, with an official letter (and entry fee) from the Newfoundland government:

> [Extract from a telegram from Rurality London to Military, St. John's, dated July 29, 1920.]
>
> Ex. 497 Robertson wishes to represent Newfoundland Olympic Marathon Antwerp August 21st Estimated expenditure 30 (pounds sterling). He has been training for three months. Entries close July 31st. Please send instructions at once.

[127] Miller, *The Official History*, 73–75.

Which was done:

> [Extract from a telegram from Military, St. John's, to Rurality London, dated July 30, 1920.]
>
> In answer to your telegram July 29th Robertson make necessary arrangements to assist entry pay expense charge this Department (Stop) Prime Minister [Richard Squires] sends to Robertson congratulations and good luck convey mine too report result.

In WWI, Newfoundland had fought as a nation. Now, Newfoundland hoped to compete as an Olympic nation. But the IOC, by its own rules, could not suddenly recognize Newfoundland and admit one of its athletes.[128] Undaunted, Robertson found his friends from the Polytechnic Harriers running club, who formed the British Olympic team. They were three (some reports say four), led by an unknown, new British record-holder for the marathon, Arthur Robert Mills (a farmer),[129] and the rules permitted one more, so Robertson was offered the remaining spot. Some form of gentleman's agreement may have helped finesse this.[130] He wore a race number for the NOC of Britain. Thus his perseverance was rewarded, and he was permitted to run.

The runners assembled in the newly built stadium (it was only finished after the start of the Games), which held the marathon's start and finish line.

The date was Sunday, August 22, and the marathon was scheduled for 4:10 pm. The day was cool and damp, sometimes raining, which made parts of the route mucky. There was some slight delay, and the starter's gun went at 4:12 pm.

[128] Fred Mason, "A 'New-found' Olympic Nation – Newfoundland's Involvement With the Olympic Games, 1904-1934," in *Proceedings: International Symposium for Olympic Research* (October 2006), 306.

[129] Martin and Gynn, *Marathon*, 98.

[130] Mason, "New-found," 306.

The route looped outside Antwerp through several villages—including Wilrijk, Reet, and Waarloos—and then reversed. They ran past Eikenhof Castle and their turnaround was the Chapel of Our Holy Virgin of the Snow, patron saint of leprosy sufferers.

The route was fairly flat. At twenty-six miles and 992 yards, it was the longest marathon designed to date. (At that time there was no standardized distance, and each Olympic organizing committee crafted their own.)

Kolehmainen placed first at a record-breaking 2:32:35.8.[131]

Thirty-three runners eventually followed Kolehmainen across the finish line before Eric Robertson finished thirty-fifth, at a time of 3:55:00, the last runner to complete the race. He was neither the only veteran nor the only former soldier to be running through his wounds. But he was probably the smallest man in the field.

Afterwards, the Harriers presented Robertson with a silver medal inscribed, "The Polytechnic Sports Club. Awarded to Eric Robertson, Olympic competitor 1920."

Colonel R. J. Kentish, a fellow marathoner from the Polytechnic, wrote from Antwerp on August 31, 1920 (on letterhead of The Army and Navy Club, Pall Mall, London):

> Dear Sir, None other than the fact that Robertson ran a very game race all through and declined to get into the ambulance which followed the Competitors in the Race although he was obviously suffering from the effects of his old wounds etc. In so doing he kept the Dominion's and the Empire's Flag flying to the end. Would you kindly see that the enclosed[132] reaches him. Yours very truly.

131 Martin and Gynn, *Marathon*, 96-107.

132 The letter addressed to Robertson, used as the epigraph to this book.

Kentish had finished thirty-five minutes before Robertson, and was his nearest competitor.

The response from the Dominion of Newfoundland High Commissioner's Offices, 58 Victoria Street, on September 4:

> Regarding the entry of Mr. Eric Robertson for the Marathon Race recently held at Antwerp, I would now confirm the latest cable dispatched to you as follows: With reference to your telegram of July 30th Robertson finished course 26 miles in three hours fiftyfive minutes thirtyfifth out of fortynine runners[133] stop winners time two hours thirtytwo and fourfifths minutes. Mr. Robertson has now returned to this county and wishes that the two letters enclosed, one addressed to this office and the other addressed to Robertson himself, may be forwarded to St. John's to describe his conduct during the race in question.[134]

The Canadian team was much taken by Robertson's desire to compete and offered to accommodate a Newfoundland athlete or athletes in 1924, in Paris, at a cost of $500 per person. But times were too hard in the Dominion, and the money could not be found.

Robertson's performance, and perhaps his simple presence, had also impressed the IOC. Newfoundland received invitations to the Games in Amsterdam in 1928, and in Los Angeles (summer) and Lake Placid (winter) in 1932. "At the request of the International Olympic Committee invitations were also sent to Malta, Rhodesia and Newfoundland," in 1928, and Newfoundland was number forty-three on

[133] In *The Olympic Marathon*, Martin and Gynn state that forty-eight runners took to the field; Kentish says there were forty-nine; in either case, only thirty-five completed the race, with Robertson the last to finish.

[134] This and other information on Robertson's health and personal and financial situation are from his Department of Veteran's Affairs file, AI-2013-00076.

the 1932 list, according to official reports.[135] But, again, Newfoundland's post-WWI economic boom had faltered. The price of fish, the prime determination of the dominion's fortunes, had fallen, and Newfoundland's bad times simply rolled along into what the rest of the world would soon experience as The Great Depression. There were no financial means to respond to the RSVP with a positive answer. While the economy was bolstered by the Second World War, Newfoundland would join Confederation in 1949, becoming part of Canada. Robertson would be the only Newfoundland-born athlete to represent his native country at the Olympics.

135 Mason, "New-found," 308.

CHAPTER TEN

A Splendid Effort

ROBERTSON NEVER TRADED on his Olympic connection. In fact, he seems to have hardly mentioned it at all.

His leg, for now, seemed healed, though his ears, which had been infected after he suffered measles as a six-year-old, were a bit of a nuisance. (Robertson would always contend that the trouble "restarted in Gallipoli.") Still he kept very active and was much involved with sports, coaching St. Bon's track and field and hockey; judging, training, and touring with a number of local track-and-field teams; and helping found the Newfoundland Amateur Athletic Association (1921).

On August 27, 1930, Robertson married Gertrude Isabel Oake at St. Thomas's Church in St. John's. Gertrude was the daughter of Jesse Oake, a merchant, and fourteen years his junior. Their daughter, Douglass, was born in 1931.

After returning to work with his father at Wholesale and Retail Dry Goods, by 1939 he had taken over the business entirely. He managed it until 1945 then he sold it, as well as his house on Bonaventure Avenue (to two of his sisters), when he, Gertrude, and Douglass emigrated to the States.

In 1949 Robertson returned to Newfoundland, alone. He was not in happy circumstances, and his downward spiral continued. Two years later, he would write the Canadian Pensions Commission:[136]

"Confidential"

24 Bonaventure Ave[137]
St. John's, Nfld
Dec 10th/1951

The Canadian Pensions Commission,

Dear Sirs,

In reference to my application, at my own request, on behalf of my wife, for allowance(s), I wish to submit the following statement.

We were married on August 27th/1930, and from that date until May 1950—I was able to support my wife, and daughter,[138] [139] substantially.

In 1945, we decided to migrate to the 'USA'.[140] We left Newfoundland on August 21st/1945,[141] arriving in New York USA, on August 22nd/1945, and proceeded from there to Waltham, Mass, to be near [142] who she lived with, for some years, before our marriage.

As soon as we got settled there, I absolutely realized that I had made a mistake, in disconnecting myself, from my friends, and business connection in St. John's, Nfld, and immediately resented the drastic change-over.

136 See Appendix 1 for the original letter.

137 Though he no longer owned the house, he was staying with his sisters.

138 Douglass.

139 These gaps due to DVA redactions.

140 Eric Robertson was 53, Gertrude 39 (birthday Dec. 8, 1906), Douglass 14.

141 These events were concurrent with the ending of WWII. Hitler's death was April 30, 1945, with German surrender May 7, and V-E Day May 8. War in the Pacific theatre continued until Japan surrendered on September 2.

142 Probably his wife's aunts, who had helped raise her.

I made a splendid effort to establish myself in Boston, with my English Woollen Agencies, (World War II, had just ended) but unfortunately for me, firms like Messrs. Jordan Marsh, Filene's,[143] Gilchrist's,[144] Sterns, and White[145] etc. had started a retrenchment programme, and were not inclined to place orders, at the very high prices prevailing at that period.

There was nothing else left but take jobs in the "low-brackets," as I had no trade, and millions of USA soldiers were returning home, to their previous positions etc.

Naturally, I worked under very trying conditions, and resented my embarrassing position, but I stuck it out, until Dec. 1948, when I returned home for the Xmas-Season. My wife followed via plane, a fortnight later, when she obtained her holidays.

During our stay in Waltham, from August 1945, to September 1946, we were allowed $100.00/xx per month, from my account in the Bank of Nova Scotia, by the Nfld Exchange Control Board,[146] which was raised to $150.00/xx per month, a few months after our arrival in Waltham, at my request, on account of the very high living conditions etc.

My wife returned to the USA from Nfld on January 6th/1949, and I followed exactly a month later, as I had some business and financial affairs to clear up.

In June 1949, we put and then my wife decided to take a position at Duxbury Mass. to get clear of the terrific heat of July and August, in Waltham.

143 Boston-based department stores, now owned by Macy's.

144 A rival Boston flagship store, now closed.

145 J. B. White, a defunct chain of stores in the southeastern US.

146 The Foreign Exchange Board was created by the Commission of Government on September 1, 1939, one of the components of the Act for the Defence of Newfoundland.

I decided to come back home for the two months, and the three of us would open up the apartment again in September 1949.

I decided to do this on the 4th of July 1949, and I got the ship at Boston on July 6th/1949. –Did not bother to get a re-entry permit, as I was fed-up, discontented, and unsettled, anyway I felt that I could fix things up with the American Authorities here in St. John's, if I decided to return, as I had my British passport etc. In the meantime, I got absolutely "run down", after severe stomach colic attacks, Neuritis,[147] Running-ears, and a terrific sun-burning, trying to knock the Neuritis out of my system, and to aggravate my condition further, my War Wounds and Varicose-veins were causing me a lot of trouble. (tough-stuff)

I arrived home, irritated, aggravated and infuriated, and ran right into the political upheaval, and like a darn fool got linked up with "the Victoria Reign die-hards" (PCs) in St. John's.

I started to get a few agencies going again to re-establish myself, and had just got going, when Confederation came along, which left me out in the cold, and shot them to pieces etc.

Before and during the political campaign, in my severe condition, I started to tip my elbow 100% (never say die) and that continued until November 1st/1949, when after putting pneumonia over on my feet, I had a bad relapse, after 10/12 days drinking, and my Doctor was forced to put me in the General Hospital, where I stayed until Dec. 29th/1949. I ended up absolutely in the Rats (chasing them) and my brain was gone, so they had to get Dr. Jerry O'Brien, from the Mental Hospital, and he gave me two/three weeks

147 Inflammation of one or more nerves.

148 LSD was another treatment for alcoholism at this time.

of Insulin injections (shock)[148] and I came out of it. – "Just like the bird." (we old soldiers are tough-stuff). This (Insulin shock) brought me back to Normal and fortunately I snapped back and have had the guts to leave Liquor alone ever since (not that it frightened me in the least—I just slipped back to the old War days, when I did not drink).

During my drinking period (the brain was gone) I drew up to nearly Six thousand dollars[149] on my business building. I decided to sell it, and fix things up, including another two thousand [in] personal accounts. I got $12,000.00 for the building—which left me finally about $3,300.00—this was a few months before I went to hospital. Well, that $3,000.00 got the Works (as I was still drinking) and the boys saw to it that it did—the tail end of it was $600.00 (Cash Cheques) during my stay at one of the hotels in the city, in 10 days; previous to going to hospital from there. The hospital bill was around $500.00, and I spent several hundred dollars playing "Santa-Claus," to the patients etc. I bet $500.00 that Mayor Carnell (late) would be re-elected, and lost it.[150] I signed a note [for] $350.00 to help out a Doctor (who was nearly as bad as I was) to get him on his feet again and got stuck for it, but he is okay now, and paying it back gradually.

When I left the hospital I had just under $1000.00 left. I struggled along, and when it got down to around $750.00 the Doctor's note came due, and he was unable to meet it, so they very nicely charged it into my account, that left me with less than $400.00. I struggled along until June 1950, when I had exactly one dollar & 62 cents left, in my account which is still open, with that handsome amount in it.

149 All 1951 amounts worth about ten times more in 2014 dollars.

150 On November 8, 1949, Harry G. Mews defeated Andrew C. Carnell for Mayor of St. John's in the general municipal election.

During the period, July 1949, to May 1950, I was sending my wife a substantial amount (I don't know how much, it is only a brain puzzler to try and think how much) to keep things going in Waltham.

Since May 1950, I have been unable to send even one dollar, as I have earned very little, and as you know that is non-support. My wife had to take a position, to live and look after our daughter, who was then in High School. The daughter [redacted] they have worked it out, somehow or other, between them.

My Wife is now 45 years old (Dec. 8th) and she is just entering a dangerous state of life, and from now on will find the going very hard, and may have to cut down work to 3/4 days a week.

There is fortunately nothing wrong between my wife and myself, and she is willing to return here, as soon as I can obtain a position, with a reasonable salary, so I can support her, and give her the standard of living, we were always used to.

I have made a great fight the last two years to adjust myself, and I have succeeded, but on account of my age, 59 (lively for my age) find it rather difficult to get placed.

Fortunately, I joined the Liberal Party in the election just over.[151] "Spontaneously", as I absolutely believe in Premier, Hon. J. R. Smallwood's "Economic Development Programme." etc., and fought for St. John's West End district. I got lots of friends in Joey's Cabinet and Party and I have no doubt that I will be placed within a reasonable time, especially when the Industries open

[151] November 26, 1951. The Liberals won 24 seats with 63.6% of the vote: the PCS 4 seats and 35.6%.

up,[152] and they know, that they can rely on me.

Now that is exactly my position at the present time and all I need is a little lift for the wife to tide her over until I can get her back here—and in the meantime I got to knock it out somehow, in spite of my War Wounds,—discharging-ears, Varicose Veins, small hernia, and a run-down Condition. I was 127 pounds last year—on Dec. 5th I tipped 107 pounds on the "DVA scales."

My only income at present is my 10% pension, $9.40 a month. $6.00 per week I get from the Doctor, and the odd resale I make around town. I got two weeks work, with the Liberal Party, and starting today (Dec. 10th) I am getting two weeks work at the General Post Office (Xmas rush).

I owe [redacted] $533.70 (arrears) board & as they have a very small income, they need it badly, and I cannot expect them, to support me.

I am receiving absolutely nothing from the DVA, or any organization, in allowances, or benefits etc.

I could write a lot more, but I guess this "episode" is to[o] long now.

I feel sure that you will give my application every consideration. (Nothing ventured, nothing won) and I sincerely hope for a little break, for my wife and myself.

Yours truly
Eric Robertson

"Confidential"

152 Smallwood's early plans for industrialization included mining iron ore in western Labrador, constructing a third pulp and paper mill in Bay D'Espoir, and opening a cement mill in Corner Brook. The Stephenville linerboard mill and Come By Chance oil refinery would also become part of this strategy.

CHAPTER ELEVEN

Pale, Frail, and a Definite Flight of Ideas

THE WAR VETERAN'S Allowance District Reviewer's Summary confirmed, "At one time he owned property valued at from ten to twelve thousand dollars," his share from the family estate. Now Robertson's "bank account shows a balance of $1.62." His appearance was described as "pale, frail, delicate strained expression...looks all of stated age," and "his past mental history poor." At fifty-nine he still listed his career as a manufacturer's agent, but at this point he was considered "permanently unemployable."

In 1951 he was living at 24 Bonaventure Avenue, noted as his sister's home. His gunshot wounds were judged "10% in extent," and he was awarded a pension based on this. Payments were effective May 30, 1951. This was the beginning of a continuous back-and-forth between Robertson and the CPC over issues of his health, pension allotments, and support for his wife.

On January 9, 1952, the War Veterans' Allowance Board investigated Robertson's W.V.A. application. This was the beginning of more than two decades of periodic and detailed assessments that would sound a similar tenor. By regular systematic routine, his identity was established by documents and personal acquaintance. It verified the story Robertson related in his letters and found "a definite financial need." A consultant's report on Robertson's psychiatric condition, submitted by C.H. Pottle, M.D., detected a history of hypomania, a mood state characterized by disinhibition and energetic talkativeness, "a definite flight of ideas."

Robertson had been "a heavy drinker," suffering "mania bouts and during these episodes has been resorting to alcohol." Pottle added a "Diagnosis (2) Manic depressive psychosis."

In December of that year, Robertson protested a clawback on his pension attributed to some short-term work as a messenger with the province's Tourist Division (then a subset of the Department of Economic Development): "I received a phone call from the Premier's[153] office that I was wanted there. I immediately went to Canada House [...] I feel I received this three months temporary employment (light work) out of sympathy."

Robertson had tried to report this, but due to some misunderstanding and the July St. George's Day holiday, the allowance was cancelled. "Why all the haste," he wrote, "I need this little increase badly & I am helping myself, in spite of all I have gone through, & I am still struggling along [...] Between the Department & Ottawa you got me 'all arsed up.'"

In this letter, Robertson also mentions that he is "trying to pay arrears of board." Although Robertson lived on Bonaventure Avenue with his sisters into the early 1950s, and seemed to list that as his address for a period after, around this time he had, as the Head of Medical Social Service later wrote,

> Gone on some kind of veteran's outing and started drinking heavily [...] At this time too, he left his sisters and boarded out [...] He pointed out that they remained very friendly and he went there for meals, but it was better for him not to live there.

[153] Joseph R. Smallwood, Premier of Newfoundland 1949-1972.

By February 1955, he was dismissed from his tourism job "due to unsatisfactory service." From this point, he never really worked again, nor did he settle into a new home. Again and again his assessments and War Veterans Allowance Investigative Reports record that he was not "presently employed," his income was "Nil," and (not unsympathetically), "It is this writer's opinion that because of his present physical condition it is doubtful whether this pensioner will be successful in obtaining work." He continued to press for coverage for his ear trouble, and in 1953 received an increase in his disability pension for this reason.

The reports of his on-and-off drinking binges continued. Another report mentions Korsakoff's syndrome, a psychiatric dementia syndrome named for Russian neuropsychiatrist Sergei Korsakoff linked to severe Vitamin B deficiency and including episodes of confabulation, of inventing memories to fill gaps in one's personal internal narrative.

He tried to obtain an advance on his pension, and a loan, from the Bank of Nova Scotia. This was brought to the attention of the Canadian Pension Committee, and they sought to administer his financial affairs "in view of this pensioner's indebtedness and recent drinking episodes."

Admitted to Lancaster Hospital in Lancaster, New Brunswick, June 28, 1956, he had bronchitis, weighted "109 (striped to the waist)," and complained of ringing in his right ear ("Get a noise in my right ear all the time"), as well as a number of other non-critical problems including swollen feet and aching legs ("The right leg is weak. Feel not too bad"). He was warned about and reprimanded for drinking.

Even from within the institution, he was still connected to his family. On June 2, 1956, it was noted, "Patient is on pass attending his daughter's wedding in the States."

He was discharged "at own request" from Ridgeway Health and Occupational Centre on March 7, 1957, and returned to Newfoundland on March 16, 1957, "very thin, and extremely talkative." His economic situation had not improved. "No bank balance. No cash on hand." Mr. Ash had written Oliver Vardy, then Director of Tourist Development, to see if there was any hope of Robertson returning to work there, but that was "impossible," Vardy replied, (using the word twice in his short letter) "as our staff is now at maximum."

Around this time, Robertson wrote a fourteen-page letter about his hearing difficulty, his penmanship much worsened by what he had endured over the few previous years, the words running uphill, and much underlined.[154]

The response, dated August 22, 1957, from Ottawa—concerning 497—Robertson, Eric—relayed that two "recent lengthy and poorly written letters have been received from this veteran, one at least obviously being written 'under the influence.' His main compliant seems to concern pension assessment for an ear condition."

Robertson's health was declining, his deterioration fueled by his drinking. In 1957, he fell down some stairs and was admitted to hospital, where he was assessed along familiar lines:

> This veteran is becoming rather more rambling in his conversation and at times would appear to have hallucinations. Still drinks whenever he has the chance. He has been separated from his wife [since 1949] but states that she would come back from Boston if he got a job and gave up drinking. Showed a letter from his wife which was certainly most friendly and showed absolutely no animosity.

In 1958 an Investigator's Report found:

[154] See Appendix 2.

> He now states he is without funds or a boarding house, and most of his clothes are at the Cleaners and different laundries. His history of boarding in this city is well known and no one risks recommending him to [the] one or two that remain [in] which he hasn't stayed. His health generally will fail if he continues in his present way of life. Domiciliary care is now his only hope of survival.

On June 17, 1958, he was re-admitted to Lancaster. "He has not been a difficult patient, but does drink from time to time," wrote the social worker. "He never gets nasty but is a great talker." One of the things he liked to talk about were his friendships within the Nova Scotian track-and-field clubs; after the war, he said he had managed different teams in Newfoundland and they often competed on mainland Canada, particularly Halifax. He talked about renewing these relationships and perhaps even his business "although, from his history I would think this would be doubtful [...] Mr. Robertson has adjusted well to hospital life but is simply getting tired of it here now."

At this point, Robertson hoped to be transferred to Camp Hill Hospital in Halifax, but this was denied, and he requested a discharge so he could return to Newfoundland. Lancaster complied but warned it "would be most reluctant to accept him back because of his alcoholism."

In 1959, P.J. Neary, Senior Pension Medical Examiner with the CPC, found, "He appeared to be neat in appearance but he is inclined to take an occasional drink." Neary thought he might now be more financially responsible, but the cheques still needed to be issued care of the District Treasury Officer, as Robertson had no fixed address.

On January 28, 1960, Robertson wrote Welfare Services, DVA. His own explanation for returning to St. John's was that he had been kept waiting so long for the transfer to Camp Hill to come through he "got fed up." Of his stay in Lancaster he said, "I stuck it out for one year and two weeks (not bad). I went through a very hard time of it (half nut crowd) but I took it occasionally opening up when forced to it. But rough as I was I never broke as much as a glass there and that's honest."

His living conditions were not good:

> Since returning home I have had a very hectic time of it. Naturally I realize that I am on my own but I'm forced to take $60.00 boarding houses (rat traps). They promise you good food and heat and as soon as you pay your board in advance all you get it soup, soup and cold—three in a room and nails driven in the wall to hang your hat on. They are all alike. I moved and moved for a better place and ran into the same everywhere—I'm really worn out. You['re] treated (soldier) as if you were a civil welfare bum, they get a fairly good show we get nothing and the works and naturally I don't stand for it. Even in the middle of the month (board in advance) I have been forced to clear out frozen to death and unnourished etc...all my clothes and laundry is outstanding. I can pick all this up if I had my cheques. At present I'm filthy, no change of anything—running on two shirts etc. and they don't even give you a drop of hot water to wash them out...I don't know exactly what to do. They are only a crowd of gold and grave diggers and money is their God.

His health was about the same: a "small thin man of very poor nutrition." He wore glasses and was very hard of hearing. He was talkative, hard to keep on track. His right leg was really hurting him, especially in the cold, and if he turned quickly he lost his balance.

He seemed to think a new environment would be best, and again he requested admittance to Camp Hill in Halifax. And he added, "I have good real friends in Ottawa." The DVA gave this implicit threat the credit they felt it deserved, but did pursue a spot at Camp Hill. Camp Hill again declined the request and suggested a return to Lancaster. But this was not acceptable to Robertson.

At sixty-eight, he stood five-foot-seven, weighed 105 pounds, and had a fair complexion and grey eyes. Doctors found him difficult to assess as he was so verbose and jumped from subject to subject. Both his legs had abrasions, probably from his stumbling into objects. He said his legs ached at night "'when the heat is turned off' by his boarding mistress." He was evaluated as needing institutional care.

He did seem to be losing capability to handle his own affairs. On July 3, 1961, CPC correspondence relates, "Mr. Robertson, who incidentally imbibes quite freely, he cashed his June pension cheque, Friday past, and for some unknown reason he either lost or mislaid $60.00 which he had set aside to pay his Board and Lodging. Mr. Robertson was asked to leave the boarding house and was successful in securing another boarding house." Both landladies involved wanted to deal with the DVA, and Robertson asked to have the office administer his pension. His residence changed constantly, counting down a rosary of low-class, even shady, addresses: Casey Street, Barter's Hill, a couple of different places on Colonial Street, the Cochrane Hotel. He moved so much he sometimes missed his cheques, and the DVA hoped he would acquire "a somewhat permanent address [...] this man is continuously moving from one boarding house to another."

Four years later he was still assessed as having "no fixed abode. He drifts from one boarding house to another, each successive one being in a poorer location and lower standard."

He was "unfit for any type of employment," and had "no car, property, or interest in business."

In January 23, 1964, he was hit by a car and taken to General Emergency where he needed some stitches to close several lacerations. He was told to return to have the sutures removed but did not do so. However, after this, things did improve. On May 7, 1964, he was accepted as a patient at the DVA Pavilion in St. John's and was approved for Domiciliary Care on June 1. He was now seventy-two.

Among the care and support he now received were regular allotments of new clothing from Ayre's Ltd.: hats, fifty-dollar suits, shirts, an overcoat, and handkerchiefs, as well as necessities like an electric razor. His health was much better attended to. His ears, for example, which had never stopped bothering him, were fitted with new hearing aids. His living conditions were better than they had been for years. He had company and he was looked after.

Robertson and his wife never reunited, but he did not forget his obligation to her. In his many, many letters to the CPC and the DVA, he always stressed her right to a portion of his pension. Their relationship was certainly cordial enough that she felt she could approach him about finances, and he always tried to push through the appropriate response.

Their correspondence[155] shows that Robertson always tried to help Gertrude. This financial support was informal as it appeared they had no court order or separation agreement, but he seemed to have great sympathy for her situation. In correspondence with CPC he continually sought to increase payments to her; at one point this "model patient" even offered to discharge himself from the DVA Pavilion if that would increase the amount going to his wife by $20 or $50.

[155] See Appendix 3 for an example of these correspondences.

He kept up his insurance payments as long as he could and the benefits were in her favour.

Many times the various officials who assessed and observed him remarked, "The veteran and his wife are on amiable terms." Gertrude continually sent him letters and kept him up-to-date and informed about her health problems, the weather, family visits: "You didn't answer my last letter, I think it was written July 7th. Did you get any work yet? I'll probably write again in a couple of weeks. Bye, love, Gertrude."

They never divorced.

Robertson died of natural causes (congestive heart failure) July 28, 1975, at the Veteran's Pavilion at General Hospital.

When Robertson died he left "cash in hand and in the bank" $6419.33. After funeral expenses—from Carnell's with burial at the General Protestant Cemetery—there was $4500, which went to his wife. His epitaph, written on a Latin Cross, reads, "Eric M Robertson, Sergeant, Royal Nfld Regiment, 28 July 1975, Age 82."

"He was generous, he wanted to share," said Dr. W. David Parsons, who knew Robertson, and helped with arrangements for his funeral. "His family were very wealthy and a fair amount of family income came to him and he spent it. He never talked about the war…He never talked about the war, and he never talked about the Olympics. He finished thirty-four or thirty-five out of fifty, but he did finish, and he was the last to finish."[156]

Indeed, in 1611 pages filed with the DVA, including summary sheets, requisition standing offer agreements, treatment activity records, applications for domiciliary care, disbursement vouchers, case sheets, discharge reports, medical examiner

[156] W. David Parsons, personal interview, 3 March, 2014.

reports, and numerous detailed personal histories, Robertson seems to have never even mentioned running the Olympic marathon.[157]

A handwritten note in his file simply reads, "Pensioner died 28-7-75, 'NF' district." No newspaper reports noted that he was one of the First Five Hundred, was wounded at Beaumont-Hamel, or the only Newfoundland-born athlete who had or would ever try to represent his once independent country at an Olympiad.

From the track at St. Bon's, to his sprint into No Man's Land at Beaumont-Hamel, through completing the full marathon course in Antwerp, throughout his continuous moves between downtown St. John's boarding houses most of the latter decades of his life, Eric Mackenzie Robertson had finished his long run.

[157] Although it may have been referenced (probably not by him) in one of his arguments with the Board of Pensions Commission, "New-found," 312, footnote 29.

APPENDIX ONE

Robertson's letter to the Pension Commission

December 10, 1951

"Confidential"

24 Bonaventure Ave
St John's. Nfld
Dec 10th/1951.

The Canadian Pension Commission,

Dear Sirs.

In reference to my application, at my own request, on behalf of my Wife, for allowances, I wish to submit the following statement.

We were married on August 27th/1930, and from that date until "May" 1950. – I was able to support my Wife, and daughter. ██████████ substantially.

In 1945, we decided to migrate to the "U.S.A." We left Newfoundland on August 21st/1945, arriving in – New York. U.S.A, on August 22nd/1945, and proceeded from there to Waltham – Mass, to be near ██████ who she lived with, for some years, before our marriage.

As soon as we got settled there, I absolutely realized that I had made a mistake, in disconnecting myself, from my friends, and business connections in St John's. Nfld, and immediately resented the drastic change-over.

I made a splendid effort to establish myself in Boston with my English Woollen Agencies. (World War II, had just ended) but unfortunately for me, firms like, Messrs. Jordan Marsh, Filene's, Gilchrists, Sterns, and Whites etc, had started a retrenchment programme, and were not incline to place orders, at the very high

000887

2/ prices prevailing at that period.

There was nothing else left but take Jobs in the "low-brackets," as I had no trade, and Millions of U.S.A. Soldiers were returning home. to their previous ~~#~~ positions etc.

Naturally. I worked under very trying conditions, and resented my embarrassing position, but I stuck it out, until Dec 1948, when I returned home for the Xmas-Season. — My Wife [redacted] followed via plane, a fortnight later, when she obtained her holidays.

During our stay in Waltham, from August 1945, to September 1946, we were allowed, \$100.00 per month, from my account in the Bank of Nova Scotia, by the Nfld Exchange Control board, which was raised to \$150.00 per Month, a few months after our arrival in Waltham, at my request, on account of the very high living-conditions etc.

My Wife [redacted] returned to the U.S.A. from Nfld on Jany 6th/1949, and I followed exactly a month later, as I had some ~~business~~ business and financial affairs to clear up.

In June 1949, we put [redacted] [redacted] and then my Wife decided to take a position at Duxbury Mass. ([redacted]) to get clear of the terrific heat of July and August. in Waltham.

I decided to come back home for the two months, and the three of us would open up the apartment again in September 1949.

I decided to do this on the 4th of July 1949. and I got the Ship at Boston on July 6th/1949. — Did not bother to get a re-entry permit, as I was fed-up, discontented and unsettled, anyway I felt that I could fix up things with the American-Authorities here in St. Johns. if I decided to return, as I had my British passport etc.

000888

3/

In the meantime, I got absolutely "run down", after severe Stomach Colic attacks, Neuritis, Running-ears, and a terrific Sun-burning, trying to knock the Neuritis out of my system, and to aggravate my condition further, my War Wounds and Varicose-veins were causing me a lot of trouble. (tough-stuff)

I arrived home, irritated, aggravated and infuriated, and ran right into the political upheaval, and like a darn fool got linked up with "the Victoria Reign die-hards" (P.C.'s) in St Johns.

I started to get a few agencies going again to re-establish myself, and had just got going, when Confederation came along which left me out in the cold, and sent them to pieces etc.

Before and during the political Campaign, in my severe condition I started to tip my elbow 100%. (never say die) and that continued until November 1st/1949, when after putting Pneumonia over on my feet, I had a bad relapse, after 10/12 days drinking, and my Docter was forced to put me in the General Hospital where I stayed until Dec. 29th/1949. - I ended up absolutely in the Rats (Chasing them) and my brain was gone, so they had to get Dr Jerry O'Brien, from the Mental Hospital and he gave me two/three weeks of Insulin-injections (Shock) and I came out of it. - "Just like the bird." (we old Soldiers, are tough-stuff) This (Insulin Shock) brought me back to Normal, and fortunately I snapped back and have had the guts to leave Liquor alone ever since. (not that it frightened me in the least, - I just slipped back to the old War days, when I did not drink)

During my drinking period (the brain was gone) I drew up to nearly Six thousand dollars, on my business building. I decided to sell it, and fix things up. including another two thousand personal accounts.

000889

4. I got $12,000.00 for the building, – which left me finally about $3,300.00 – this was a few months before I went to hospital.

Well, that $3,300.00 got the works (as I was still drinking) and the boys saw to it that it did. – The tail end of it was $600.00 (Cash Cheques) during my stay at one of the hotels in the City in 10 days: previously to going to hospital from there.

The hospital bill was around $500.00, and I spent several hundred dollars playing "Santa-Claus" to the patients etc. I bet $500.00 that Mayor Carnell (late) would be re-elected and lost it.

I signed a Note $350.00 to help out a Doctor (who was nearly as bad as I was) to get him on his feet again and got stuck for it, but he is okay now and paying it back gradually.

When I left the hospital I had just under $1,000.00 dollars left. I struggled along and when it got down to around $750.00 the Doctors note came due, and he was unable to meet it, so they very nicely charged it into my account, that left me with less than $400.00. – I struggled along until June 1950 when I had exactly one dollar + 62 cents left, in my account which is Stell open with that handsome amount in it.

During the period, July 1949, to May 1950, I was sending my Wife substantial amounts (I don't know how much it is only a brain puzzler to try and think how much) to keep things going in Waltham.

Since May 1950, I have been unable to send even one dollar, as I have earned very little, and as You know that is Non-support. – My Wife had to take a position, to live and look after our daughter, who was then in High School. –

000890

5.

The daughter, [redacted]

they have knocked it out, somehow or other, between them.

My Wife is now 45 years old (Dec 8th) and she is just entering a dangerous state of Life. and from now on will find the going very hard. and may have to cut down work to 3/4 days a week.

There is fortunately nothing wrong between my Wife and myself, and she is willing to return here, as soon as I can obtain a position, with a reasonable salary, so as I can support her, and give her the standard of living we were always use to.

I have made a great fight the last two years to adjust myself, and I have ~~succeeded~~ succeeded. but on account of my age. 59. (lively for my age) find it rather difficult to get placed.

Fortunately, I joined the Liberal Party in the election just over "Spontaneously": as I absolutely believe in Premier, Hon J. R. Smallwood's "Economic development programme": etc. and fought for St. John's West End. district. — I got lots of friends in Joey's Cabinet and Party and I have no doubt, that I will be placed within a reasonable time, especially when the Industries open up. and they know, that they can rely on me.

Now. that is exactly my position at the present time and all I need is a little lift. for the wife to tide her over until I can get her back here. and in the meantime I got to knock it out somehow. in spite of my War Wounds. —

000891

6.
discharging - ears. Varicose Veins. small hernia. and a run-down - Condition. I was 127 pounds last year - On Dec 5th - I tipped. 107 pounds. on the "DVA - scales".

My only income at present. is my 10% pension. $9.40 a month. $6.00 per week. I get from that Doctor. and the odd. resale I make around town. - I got two weeks work. with the Liberal - Party. and starting today (Dec 10th) I am getting two weeks work. at the General Post Office (Xmas rush)

I owe [redacted] $533.70 (arrears) board. & as they have a very small income. they need it badly. and I cannot expect them, to support me.

I am receiving absolutely nothing from the DVA, or any organization. in allowances. or benefits etc.

I could write a lot more, but I guess this "episode" is too long now.

I feel sure that you will give my application every consideration. (Nothing Ventured, Nothing Won) and I sincerely hope for a little break. for my Wife and myself.

[illegible]

Eric Robertson

Confidential

000892

APPENDIX TWO

Excerpt from Robertson's letter to the Pension Commission

August 10, 1957

2 You good people got the Works, instead of someone else —

Anyway I told the truth & I know you gentlemen will forgive me

I may not remember all I wrote but even in my drunks I was Full absolutely Full Rum & Stout & Wine & good mixtures (and S.P. & like the Bird today) & its only the Canadian Divison & the Royal Regt (The old 500) that can do that BROTHER. come around quick & keep at 65 years old

I'm picking up for Jes Gares under Dr Gallagher's care He is Wonderful & he

000320

3 Federal Govt were wise in
Capturing [redacted] a man like Ewing
(He is a great friend to
all Veterans) & also
Lawyer. 7 O'Dea
Be sure Joy keep them
To Real Kindly Gentlemen &
we need them HERE
My Hearing is absolutely
Lousy I can hear
yes but I cannot
make out one word of
the Normal Voice
I can hear & I cannot
hear — All I want is
an opportunity to get things
going yes Molly is
due Feb here on
August 18th then see

000321

APPENDIX THREE

Correspondances regarding the distribution of Robertson's pension 1964–1966

Mrs. Gertrude Robertson,
303 Newton Street,
Waltham, Massachusetts,
U. S. A.

Re: #497 - ROBERTSON, Eric McKenzie

Dear Madam:-

This is to inform you that after a recent review of your husband's case, the Commission has ruled to pay the additional pension for yourself, together with an equivalent portion of your husband's personal pension to you direct, with effect from the date of the last payment.

The Chief Treasury Officer will adjust your account and send you a statement in due course.

Yours faithfully,

WGB:FA
BUFF/St.John's,Nfld.

WGB

for Secretary.

P.M.E.

The Commission has further ruled to pay the balance of pension for administration under the direction of the Senior Pension Medical Examiner at the District Office.

Monday Dec. 13, 1965.

Dear Eric.

Thank you so very much for my birthday card, Christmas card and the ten dollars. I need my hair done. I'm going to get a permanent, so will use the ten for that. was so pleased with the forty dollars you sent them for Christmas. I was most grateful that you remembered.

Eric, can you please send me some money each month. I am now working only part time, three days a week. The arthritis in my back is gradually becoming worse and its now in my left ankle as well.

I can't make ends meet on three days pay. My rent is now ninety dollars ($90) per month, with phone, light and gas brings it up to $105.00 a month. The pension check is reduced to $83.33 because of the rate of exchange.

Dr. Adams said rest was what I needed for arthritis and you know he's so right, becasue nearly a month ago I was sick for two weeks with the flu, spent eleven days in bed running a high fever for a week and my back didn't bother me at all.

Don't give your money away Eric, I need it. I'm your wife and your responsibility. I've worked so hard for the past twenty years I8m worn out. Will you please write to me, tell me what you can do.

Have a nice Christmas at and a good New Year.

With love,

Gertrude.

CERTIFIED TRUE COPY
29-12-65 M. Dyke

Pension No. 261091

THE CANADIAN PENSION COMMISSION

Rank .... Unit ROY. NFLD. REGT. (WW 1)

Name ROBERTSON: Eric M. Service No. 497

Relationship of applicant for Pension to member of forces ....

Present Pension Status

Date January 21, 1966

Pension is in payment at 70% with additional pension for wife.

The pension is divided. The additional pension on behalf of the wife in the amount of $44.80 together with an equivalent portion of the pensioner's personal pension, making a total payment of $89.60, is being paid to the wife who resides in Waltham, Mass., the balance of the pension is being paid to the District Office for administration on behalf of the pensioner.

At the present time the pensioner is a Domiciliary Care patient under Section 29 VTR in St. John's General Hospital.

The Commission's attention is invited to their decision dated September 29, 1964 at which time the present division of pension was placed in effect.

The wife wrote to the pensioner on December 13, 1965 thanking him for the birthday card and Christmas card as well as the money that was sent to her. The wife also asked the pensioner as to whether it was possible for him to send some additional money each month. The wife stated that she was working only part-time - three days a week. She stated that the arthritis in her back was gradually becoming worse and is now in her left ankle. The wife stated that she can't make ends meet on three days pay. Her rent is $90.00 per month plus phone, light and gas bringing the total expenditure up to $105.00 per month. She stated that the pension cheque she receives is reduced to $83.33 because of the rate of exchange.

The pensioner called at the District Office requesting that her part of his pension be increased. It is stated that the pensioner appears to be very concerned about his wife's circumstances and asked the District Office to request the Commission to increase his wife's portion of pension by $50.00 a month.

In addition to the pension payments the pensioner is also in receipt of Old Age Security of $75.00 per month.

As the pensioner is a Domiciliary Care patient the case was referred to Treatment Entitlement for their comments. Treatment Services have no objection if the Commission decide to increase the amount going forward to the wife by an additional $15.00 per month. They will still be able to recover full maintenance charges under Section 29 VTR from the pensioner's income. Treatment Services are of the opinion that if the pensioner wishes to give his wife additional funds he could release monies from his personal Trust Fund.

The instructions of the Commission are requested please as to whether it will be in order to pay the additional pension on behalf of the wife together with $59.80 per month of the pensioner's personal pension, making a total payment of $104.60 to the wife with the balance of the pension in the amount of $80.20 to the District Office for administration on behalf of the pensioner.

PTO.

Signed at Ottawa .... January 25, 1966.

(Chairman) Canadian Pension Commission

(Member) Canadian Pension Commission

(Member) Canadian Pension Commission

EWB/DC EWB:AK

C.P.C. 566 (Rev. 2-57)

000078

SOURCES

"The Origin of the 3rd L.G.H...Reprinted from The Gazette of the 3rd London General Hospital, February 1917." *The WWI Document Archive*, accessed July 2014. http://www.vlib.us/medical/wandswth/wandswth.htm.

Ashworth, Tony. "The Live and Let Live Syndrome." In *The World War I Reader*, edited by Michael S. Neiberg, 386-418. New York: New York UP, 2007.

Beckett, Ian F. *The Making of the First World War*. New Haven: Yale University Press, 2012.

Brittain, Vera. "Letters from a Lost Generation." In *The World War I Reader*, edited by Michael S. Neiberg, 420-452. New York: New York UP, 2007.

-----. "Return of a Dead Officer's Kit." *The Guardian*, 14 November 2008. http://www.theguardian.com/world/2008/nov/14/first-world-war-vera-brittain.

Brown, Malcolm, ed. *Meeting in No Man's Land: Christmas 1914 and Fraternization in the Great War*. London: Constable, 2007.

Copp, Terry, and Mark Osborne Humphries. *Combat Stress in the 20th Century: The Commonwealth Perspective*. Kingston: Canadian Defence Academy Press, 2010.

Curtis, Richard, Ben Elton, Rowan Atkinson, and John Lloyd. *Blackadder: The Whole Damn Dynasty, 1485-1917*. London: Penguin, 2000.

Ferguson, Niall. *The Pity of War*. New York: Basic Books, 1999.

Gold, John R., and Margaret M. Gold, eds. *Olympic Cities: City Agendas, Planning and the World's Games, 1896-2012*. New York: Routledge, 2007.

Hadley, Frederick, and Martin Legler. *Posters of the Great War*. South Yorkshire: Pen and Sword Military, 2013.

Howard, Michael. *The First World War: A Very Short Introduction*. London: Oxford UP, 2002.

Jones, Heather. "Prisoners of War." *The British Library*, accessed September 2014. http://www.bl.uk/world-war-one/articles/prisoners-of-war.

MacDonald, Gayle. "A Picture of PTSD." *The Globe and Mail*, June 9, 2014.

Major, Kevin. Interview with the author. June 26, 2014.

-----. *No Man's Land: A Play*. St. John's: Pennywell Books, 2005.

Martin, David E., and Roger W.H. Gynn. *The Olympic Marathon*. Champaign, Ill: Human Kinetics, 2000.

Mason, Fred. "A 'New-found' Olympic Nation—Newfoundland's Involvement with the Olympic Games, 1904-1934." In *Proceedings: International Symposium for Olympic Research*, October, 2006.

Miller, David. *The Official History of the Olympic Games and the IOC*. Edinburgh: Mainstream Publishing, 2012.

Neiberg, Michael S., ed. *The World War I Reader*. New York: New York UP, 2007.

Nicholson, Colonel G.W.L. *The Fighting Newfoundlander: A History of the Royal Newfoundland Regiment*. Montreal: McGill-Queen's UP, 2006.

O'Neill, Paul. *The Oldest City: The Story of St. John's, Newfoundland*. St. John's: Boulder, 2003.

Parsons, W. David. "The Importance of Beaumont Hamel." Unpublished paper, Centre for Newfoundland Archives, QE II Library, Memorial University, 2014.

-----. personal interview. March 3, 2014.

Philip Gubbs, "The Historic First of July." In *The World War I Reader*, edited by Michael S. Neiberg, 185-190. New York: New York UP, 2007.

Rowland, David. *The Stress of Battle: Quantifying Human Performance in Combat*. London: TSO, 2006.

Simkin, John. "Football and The First World War." *Spartacus Educational*, accessed August 2015. http://spartacus-educational.com/FWWfootball.htm.

Sweet, Barb. "Service Monday Will Remember the Arrival of the 1914 War Telegram," *The Telegram*, August 2, 2014.

Terret, Thierry, and J.A. Mangan, eds. *Sport, Militarism and the Great War*. London: Routledge, 2012.

Todman, Dan. *The Great War: Myth and Memory*. London: Hambledon and London, 2005.

Trueman, Chris. "The Home Front 1914 to 1918." *The History Learning Site*. http://www.historylearningsite.co.uk/home_front_1914_to_1918.htm.

Verhey, Jeffrey. "'War Enthusiasm': Volunteers, Departing Soldiers, and Victory Celebrations." In *The World War I Reader*, edited by Michael S. Neiberg, 279-297. New York: New York UP, 2007.

Wilhelm of Germany to Nicholas II of Russia. "The Willy-Nicky Telegrams." In *The World War I Reader*, edited by Michael S. Neiberg, 88-93. New York: New York UP, 2007.

Winter, Jay, and Jean-Louis Robert, eds. *Capital Cities at War: Paris, London, Berlin 1914-1918*. Cambridge: Cambridge UP, 1997.

Information on Eric Robertson's health and personal and financial situation are sourced from his Department of Veteran's Affairs file: AI-2013-00076.

ACKNOWLEDGEMENTS

I would like to thank Iain McCurdy and Edward Riche for their thoughts and insight given to earlier drafts of the manuscript. Thanks to James and Rhonda at Breakwater Books. And thanks to Bert Riggs for bringing this, and so many other great Newfoundland stories, to our attention.

JOAN SULLIVAN is the editor of the *Newfoundland Quarterly*. As a freelance journalist, her interviews, reviews, and commentary have appeared in *The Telegram*, *The Globe and Mail*, and on CBC Radio's *Tapestry*. As a playwright, director, and actor, Sullivan has worked with the Atlantic Fringe Festival in Halifax, the National Arts Centre in Ottawa, and the Document Theatre Collective in St. John's. Her book *In the Field*, about Stephen Norris of the Royal Newfoundland Regiment, won the 2013 Rogers Communications Award for Non-Fiction. She lives in St. John's.